The
Bright
Hour

a memoir of living and dying

NINA RIGGS

Simon & Schuster

New York   London   Toronto   Sydney   New Delhi

Simon & Schuster
1230 Avenue of the Americas
New York, NY 10020

First Simon & Schuster hardcover edition June 2017

SIMON & SCHUSTER and colophon are registered trademarks
of Simon & Schuster, Inc.

For information about special discounts for bulk purchases, please
contact Simon & Schuster Special Sales at 1-866-506-1949 or
business@simonandschuster.com.

The Simon & Schuster Speakers Bureau can bring authors to your live event. For
more information or to book an event, contact the Simon & Schuster Speakers
Bureau at 1-866-248-3049 or visit our website at www.simonspeakers.com.

Interior design by Carly Loman

Manufactured in the United States of America

10   9   8   7   6   5   4   3   2   1

Library of Congress Cataloging-in-Publication Data

Names: Riggs, Nina, author.
Title: The bright hour : a memoir of living and dying / Nina Riggs.
Description: New York : Simon & Schuster, 2017.
Identifiers: LCCN 2017007161| ISBN 9781501169359 (hardback) | ISBN
 9781501169373 (trade paper) | ISBN 9781501169366 (ebook)
Subjects: LCSH: Riggs, Nina. | Riggs, Nina—Philosophy. |
 Breast—Cancer—Patients—United States—Biography. | Terminally
 ill—United States—Biography. | Death. | Life. | Death—Psychological
 aspects. | Mothers—United States—Biography. | Women poets,
 American—Biography. | BISAC: BIOGRAPHY & AUTOBIOGRAPHY / Personal
 Memoirs. | BIOGRAPHY & AUTOBIOGRAPHY / Women. | BIOGRAPHY &
 AUTOBIOGRAPHY / Medical.
Classification: LCC RC280.B8 R5355 2017 | DDC 362.19699/4490092 [B] —dc23
LC record available at https://lccn.loc.gov/2017007161

ISBN 978-1-5011-6935-9
ISBN 978-1-5011-6936-6 (ebook)

for my boys: John, Freddy, and Benny
and
in memory of my mom, Janet Angela Riggs, 1947–2015

I am cheered with the moist, warm, glittering, budding and melodious hour that takes down the narrow walls of my soul and extends its pulsation and life to the very horizon. That is morning; to cease for a bright hour to be a prisoner of this sickly body and to become as large as the World.

RALPH WALDO EMERSON, 1838

Prologue: The Bike Ride

"Dying isn't the end of the world," my mother liked to joke after she was diagnosed as terminal.

I never really understood what she meant, until the day I suddenly did—a few months after she died—when, at age thirty-eight, the breast cancer I'd been in treatment for became metastatic and incurable. There are so many things that are worse than death: old grudges, a lack of self-awareness, severe constipation, no sense of humor, the grimace on your husband's face as he empties your surgical drain into the measuring cup.

My husband, John, and I were on the sidewalk in front of the house, our bodies moving together in the late morning sun, teaching our younger son to ride a bike.

"Don't let me go yet!" Benny was hollering.

"But you've got it, you've got it," I keep saying, running along beside him. I can feel a new steadiness in his momentum under my grip of the back of his seat. "You're practically doing it all on your own."

"But I'm not ready!" he yells.

We never taught our older son, Freddy, to ride. One day he begged to take the training wheels off, and minutes later was riding laps around the backyard. Not Benny. He is never ready for us to let go.

"Do you have me?" he keeps asking.

The weekend air is a medicine, and I'm starting to feel stronger and stronger: months of chemo behind me, close to finishing six weeks of radiation. We're aiming for the stop sign at the corner—maybe fifty feet ahead—with the slightest incline.

"Strong legs," John is saying. "Steady eyes, steady handlebar."

A young couple with a dog crosses the street to get out of our way. They smile at Benny. I'm smiling at them and trying to catch John's eye. He's going to do it. I'm not looking down. I'm looking ahead.

Then: my toe catches, and I stumble on a lip in the cement.

In that moment, something snaps deep within. Benny hears me yelp, and John and I both let go of him. John is supporting my whole weight and I'm floating somewhere in the new universe called Pain. But I'm also watching Benny wobbling forward. He keeps going and going.

"I'm sorry, Mom! Are you okay?" he is yelling over his shoulder. "Look! I'm still riding!"

And there it is: The beautiful, vibrant, living world goes on.

The next day at the hospital, inside the MRI machine, where it sounded like hostile aliens had formed a punk band, I was reminded of a story I heard on NPR about a team-building exercise that an employer in South Korea was using to raise worker morale.

During the exercise, the employees dress in long robes and sit at desks. Each writes a letter to a loved one as if it were their last correspondence. Sniffling and even outright weeping are acceptable. Next to each desk is a big wooden box. But not an ordinary wooden box; a coffin.

When the workers are done with the letter, they lie down in the coffin and someone pretending to be the Angel of Death comes around and hammers the top shut. They lie in the dark inside the coffin as still as they can be for about ten minutes. The idea is that when they emerge from the pretend burial they will have a new perspective, one that will make them more passionate about their work and appreciative of their lives.

All around me: Rooms of gowned patients were lying flat on their backs inside tight loud tubes and silent patients were wheeled to and from these darkened basement rooms. We are practicing, I thought. As the machine clanked and buzzed for over an hour, I became the Angel of Stillness. I thought: Forget the Angel of Death. The contrast dye sizzled in my veins, and just as the tech warned me, the Angel of Medical Imaging came close but never touched me. When the noise finally stopped, I could hear the voice of a different machine in some nearby room instructing: BREATHE. STOP BREATHING. NOW BREATHE.

In the MRI control room, a picture was surfacing out of the dark of the screen: my spine being devoured by a tumor. They call the break *pathologic*—caused by underlying disease. This was the MRI where they found that the cancer had spread to my bones. This was the MRI that suggested I had eighteen to thirty-six months to live.

A half hour later I would be lying in the same position in a curtained emergency room bay being told by a teary radiation oncology resident—squeezing my hand, patting my bald head—that the pain I'd been having for two months, which I'd been assured was from having a weak core after months of chemo, was actually from the cancer that now would never go away.

STAGE ONE

1. One Small Spot

The call comes when John is away at a conference in New Orleans. Let's not linger on the thin light sifting into our bedroom as I fold laundry, the last leaves shivering on the willow oak outside — preparing to let go but not yet letting go. The heat chattering in the vent. The dog working a spot on her leg. The new year hanging in the air like a question mark. The phone buzzing on the bed.

It's almost noon. Out at the school, the kids must be lining up for recess, their fingers tunneling into their gloves like explorers.

Cancer in the breast, the doctor from the biopsy says. *One small spot.* One small spot. I repeat it to John, who steps out of a breakout session when he sees my text. I repeat it to my mom, who says, "You've got to be kidding me. Not you, already."

I repeat it to my dad who shows up at my house with chicken soup. I repeat it to my best friend, Tita, and she repeats it to me as we sit on the couch obsessing over all twenty words of the phone conversation with the doctor. I repeat it brushing my teeth, in the carpool line, unclasping my bra, falling asleep, walking the aisles of the grocery store, walking on the greenway, lying in the cramped, clanky cave of the MRI machine while they take a closer look. *One small spot.*

It becomes a chant, a rallying cry. One small spot is fixable.

One small spot is a year of your life. No one dies from one small spot.

"Oh, breast cancer," I remember my great-aunt saying before she died at age ninety-three of heart failure. "That's something I did in the 1970s."

2. World of Trouble

Several weeks before the call, a warm night: John and I sit on the front porch with glasses of whiskey and let the sun set in our eyes— bathing us and the whole world in orange as it sinks below the neighbor's roofline across the street where he's out on his swing— the retired professor who can no longer remember his dog's name. His wife flickers at the kitchen window, and he nods toward us. The only sky he sees is the dark that's coming.

A *world of trouble* is what I told our kids to expect if they left their beds to follow us out here.

3. The Punnett Square

"My paternal grandfather had breast cancer."

That tends to make whoever is charting my medical history look up. "He had a radical mastectomy in the 1970s. And his sister had it, too—she died in her fifties. And one of his nieces. And his daughter—my aunt."

I'm sitting in the genetic counselor's office as she madly sketches out my family tree on a sheet of paper. There are squares and circles, the cancer victims marked with X's. Lots of X's.

On my mom's side: cancer in both her parents, although not breast. An early melanoma in her sister. And less than six months after this conversation, my mom herself will be dead from a blood cancer called multiple myeloma.

As the genetic counselor is drawing the diagrams, I am remembering a similar one from seventh-grade science class, the Punnett square: almost fortune-teller-like, better than Ouija boards and those folded-up cootie-catchers—when the grown-up self is almost equally conceivable and impossible. Pick any boy in the class, and you could predict the likelihood that you and he would have kids with brown eyes or hair on their toes and fingers. Or—as the genetic counselor's diagram seems to suggest—cancer.

According to the Punnett square, two kids at my table, Mike Henninger and Christina Stapleton, had a 100 percent chance of having a blue-eyed baby. This thrilled seventh-grade me: Something about the future was settled, then. A certainty—if Christina and Mike fall in love. And want a child. And Christina is able to get pregnant. And the baby arrives safely into the world.

On my dad's side: His older sister has the breast cancer mutation BRCA2. She was the first of us to be tested, after her diagnosis in the 1990s. Her daughter, who has not had cancer, also has the mutation. And so does at least one of my dad's three living brothers.

But it turns out I do not have it. I have just been diagnosed with breast cancer at age thirty-seven, but I do not have the breast cancer mutation.

"I'm going to send you a study I found," the genetic counselor tells me. "You might be interested in the findings, given your situation."

Researchers have discovered that in families where there is an identified breast-cancer-gene mutation such as BRCA1 or BRCA2, even family members without the mutation are at a greater risk for developing the disease.

"All this likely means is that there are some genes we have not successfully mapped yet," the counselor says. "We are seeing part of the picture, but not all of it."

We are certain only that there is so much of which we are not certain.

As far as we know now, genetics accounts for only about 11 percent of all breast cancers. Which leaves 89 percent hurtling randomly toward us through outer space.

My grandfather, the one with breast cancer, died when I was seven, two years after my grandmother. Cancer, both of them—his

maybe metastasized from the breast, maybe something else. We can't be sure—it was the early 1980s.

"Did you ever see his scars," asks one of my uncles after my diagnosis, "from the mastectomy?"

Once I did, although at the time I thought they were from a war. It was summer. I was five or six years old and we were down on the rocky beach below our family summer house on Cape Cod, where my grandmother's horse, Sachem, had caught a leg between two large rocks, snapped it with the force of his own heaving and had to be shot. The horse's body was too immense to move, and everyone was sweating from the work of covering him with a mound of rocks piled taller than me.

My grandfather's body was lean and muscled and rigid—the familiar family physique—but his bare chest was another planet: distorted, twisted with scar tissue, hollowed out to the rib cage like a wooden-hulled skiff.

Grown-ups are full of surprises, I remember thinking. *Who could ever possibly imagine what it is to be one?*

Years later, farther down the beach where the bluff curls to a weedy cove, some of Sachem's bones eventually returned to us—bleached, worn, and so massive at first I imagined they belonged to a prehistoric beast. Now one is kept on the table near the mantel, next to the angry jaw of a bluefish, the slough of a king snake, a brittle helix of thousands of conch eggs and two wooden plaques carved with my grandparents' dates.

Some things are meant to return to us again and again.

4. Nothing Good

"I don't think I can tell the boys until I can get my head around it myself," I say to my mom the day after the diagnosis. Freddy has just turned eight, and Benny is five.

"Okay," she says, "but just know that no time is going to be the perfect time."

Eight years earlier, when my mom called me from the doctor's office after her diagnosis of multiple myeloma, I was sitting on the edge of my bed, nursing the baby. He was two weeks old.

"Goddammit, I am so furious that this is happening," I remember her saying.

I didn't cry. I told her not to worry, to focus on driving home safely, and that I would call my brother, Charlie, who was away at college. But when it was time for me to be the bearer of the news, I could hardly speak.

"What are you trying to say?" Charlie kept asking.

"Nothing good," was the best I could do.

Thankfully, he got it with only a few questions. I didn't move from the edge of the bed for a long time. My baby was milk-drunk in my lap, and his onesie was soaked through.

5. *www.heyninariggseverythingisgoingtobeok.com*

The kids are out of school the Monday after my diagnosis, so John takes the day off to try to keep them out of the house while I get my head around it. I lie on my back in bed, imagining being a sick person. *What do sick people think about? How do you know when you start to be a sick person?*

I'm also wondering about this unfamiliar calm that has settled over me in the last several days—ever since the doctor on the phone spoke the word *cancer*. At the same time as I have watched the terror build in John's eyes, I have felt somehow relieved. *It has happened*, I keep thinking. *The terrible thing. This is what the terrible thing feels like.* Somehow, a lovely space has opened up inside my chest, a little, deep pool in the thickest woods.

An earlier version of me—even me from a week ago—is already googling my way to a PhD on breast cancer death rates. Over the past decade I have earned my Google PhD in at least a hundred catastrophic topics—usually fates that could befall my poor children: chance of death by undetected rabies bite, chance of death by green-tinged diarrhea, chance of death by large ear lobes, chance of death due to eating playground mulch, chance of death due to an unnatural passion for ceiling fans and kitty cats.

I remember once reading that ovarian cancer very often went undetected because patients did not have any obvious symptoms

14

early on. *I also have no obvious symptoms*, I was able to deduce, *so clearly I have ovarian cancer.*

John shakes his head: "You're amazingly crazy," he says. "You know—for not being crazy." Since I was a little girl, I have planned an escape route whenever I sleep in a bed that isn't my own. John doesn't worry about anything until the rooms are full of smoke and someone is shaking him and flames are licking under the door: *Okay fine, maybe we should call 911.*

Darkest confession: One time, alone with the baby for too many hours—the day already dark, John still at the office—I knowingly let nine-month-old Freddy repeatedly suck on the power cord to my laptop—he giggled and whined simultaneously each time it zapped his tongue—so that I could have a spare second to scour the Internet for something that would tell me the likelihood of a healthy, verbally precocious nine-month-old developing autism.

A couple years back, when a therapist helped me realize through a series of exercises that the only thing that would satisfy me on the Internet was a website that explicitly said: "Freddy and Benny are going to be just fine. So are you and John," I laughed out loud at myself. But it didn't really stop me from seeing disaster at every corner, or checking from time to time to make sure the magical website did not in fact exist.

"You're holding on so tight," that therapist told me. "You think you will be obliterated if anything bad ever happens."

Now, lying in my bed, obliteration feels like peace, like drifting toward sleep. *This is the terrible thing.*

Meanwhile, John and the kids go to the park, to Target, to the library. When they get home, John comes upstairs quietly and sits down on the end of the bed. "I need to talk to you," he says.

"Okay," I say.

"I really wish I didn't have to say this, so try not to freak out."

"Okay," I say again.

"I think Freddy has developed diabetes." John has been a type-one diabetic for nearly twenty years. They said it's not genetic. . . .

"Okay." I absolutely cannot think of one other thing to say.

"I noticed he was drinking a lot from the water fountain at the library, and it reminded me of when I was diagnosed. So I tested his blood sugar on my meter. It's off the charts."

"Okay."

"There's really nothing else it could be," he says.

With hardly any more words, I put my clothes on, and we pack up the car and call the pediatrician and head to the hospital. Freddy's eyes are scared and exhausted.

"It completely sucks," I say, pulling him against me as we walk out to the car. "But trust me: You're going to survive."

On the way to the hospital I get a call that my MRI results have come in. We stop by the Breast Center, part of the same complex. The woman at reception hands me the test results and a large pink tote bag. "Complimentary!" she says.

One small spot, the printout confirms. I can breathe again and then I can't as we walk onto the children's ward, the pink tote over my shoulder.

Freddy is a great sport at the hospital, but he hates it when they put in the IV, which takes a number of sticks in his tiny hand, and he's not shy about letting the nurses know.

"I'm surprised you're okay with doing something so painful to a kid," he tries, incensed by the multiple attempts. And: "Are you sure you have actually put in an IV before?" And: "Isn't there some other patient you should be helping right now?"

The saintly nurse rolls her eyes, and John heads out to get Freddy some chicken wings and broth from his favorite Chinese restaurant—something with low carbohydrates that won't further elevate his blood sugar. While he's gone I call my mom.

"I know it's going to sound like I'm making this up," I say.

First I tell her the news from my MRI, then Freddy's diagnosis. They want to keep us here for three to four days—to get his blood sugar under control, stabilize his kidneys, teach us how to give him shots—even though John is already a pro.

Benny isn't allowed to stay on the ward because it's flu season, so John takes him home after dinner. We talk on the phone later that night.

"I really didn't want to tell you," John says. "In fact, I considered taking him straight to the hospital and telling you I'd decided to take the kids on an impromptu trip. It just seemed really important not to let you find out."

Freddy's asleep at last. I'm lying nearby on the foldout chair, lights off in the hospital room—just the flash of the heart monitor, sending out a steady code into the night like a lighthouse: *okay for now, okay for now, okay for now.*

"I'm so glad it was you who was on parent patrol," I say. "I think it would have sailed past me. I kind of feel like I've had a lobotomy."

"Oh yeah, I wasn't going to tell you that part either, but I had them take care of that as well," he says. "It seemed for the best."

6. *Nonplussed*

The Queen of Triple Negative Breast Cancer: that's the doctor I have the great fortune of being squeezed in to see so she can determine how to treat this aggressive-seeming, hormone-negative tumor, the clinic coordinator at Duke Cancer Center tells me.

John and I take a selfie in the exam room while we wait.

"This is what two completely terrified people who are trying to act like they've got it all under control look like," I say, showing it to him.

"How many people do you think are going to feel you up today?" he says.

The first appointment is at 9:20 a.m., and we don't leave the clinic until 6:00 p.m. Dr. Cavanaugh is smart like a switchblade and wears knee-high black boots with her white coat. She looks completely together. She might be my polar opposite.

She seems to terrify everyone around her, and John and I both love her right away. She knows the details of my case off the top of her head. She refers to my cancer as being "highly curable." She says she prefers to call chemo combinations "recipes" because "cocktail" makes her think about having a drink too early in the day and that's disappointing. So maybe we are not polar opposites.

"I like how nonplussed she seems by the whole thing," I say to John after she leaves the room and I'm wiggling back into my sports bra. There is still a huge bruise on my breast from the biopsy, and I have to keep reminding myself that it is not the tumor—just a side effect. "She's totally unimpressed by my cancer. Maybe even a little bored by it. I think that's good."

"I don't think nonplussed means what you think it means," says John, half listening to a work voicemail he's missed.

"Really?" I say. My shirt is inside out. He helps me pull it back over my head. "Doesn't it mean blasé—like not worked up about something?"

"It's the opposite." Now he's groping around under my shirt with one hand as he googles the word on his phone with the other. "I don't believe you," I say. He shows me the definition.

"Oh," I say, pushing his hand away. "Then I like how non-nonplussed she is. And I am frankly nonplussed by your behavior in this exam room."

The rest of the day: scans, waiting, talking to pharmacists, more waiting, and meeting the rest of the team—the radiation oncologist, the surgeon. The surgeon makes me smile when he makes a Freudian slip while referring to the choice between lumpectomy and mastectomy as being "my incision" instead of "my decision."

7. At Chemo School

Everyone is fiercely upbeat as we learn not to eat rare tuna and how to tie a square scarf and what kind of mouthwash is good for mouth ulcers.

I sit with a friendly-faced nurse and a number of other newly diagnosed folks in their seventies and eighties, crowded around a table in the bowels of the cancer center. There are so very many of us, actually, I might be suffocating.

"Are we having fun yet?" asks an abundantly lipsticked lady as she fiddles with her cane.

"I know I am!" pipes up her husband, grinning at the nurse, then me.

I text Tita, who had offered to come with me. "Now I really wish you had come. You would adore this scene." She is a fiction writer, and she loves the inner workings of things: bodies, minds, relationships, support group meetings. She loves to pull things apart and examine every weird corner of them. We can spend hours dissecting a strange interaction at the grocery store or a waiter's mannerisms or the emotional challenges her sister's ex-boyfriend's mother might be facing. "I feel like I've been granted access to the mecca of unexpected intimacy," I say.

"PLEASE. WRITE. EVERY. SINGLE. THING. DOWN," she texts back.

The nurse emphasizes the importance of condom use during

midchemo sexual intercourse and everyone stares in my direction. I take furious notes in my binder. I underline condom twice, maybe three times.

"I have the c-word but the c-word doesn't have me," someone says and we all nod.

Discussing the chemo shellfish prohibition, a gray-faced man in a golf jacket announces that he has a "sexual attraction to pulling the shell off shrimp by the tail."

"Oh for God's sake—this again," moans his wife. After a big pause, everyone laughs for real.

We recite the cancer center phone number aloud in unison, with gusto. We wish each other well.

We graduate. We're ready for the big leagues.

8. In the Chemo Bay

The treatment room has no doors. Maybe a pulled curtain, a hushed voice, but in the end it is an open sea of people waiting together to take in the poisonous stuff that we hope will make us better. Time moves differently here—so much waiting, so much taking place. All the double-checking and bracelet scanning. All the side effect management: Zofran, steroids, saline flushing. The *please-repeat-your-name-and-birth-date. Do you need a snack? More water?* The keen eyes of the hazmat-suited nurses, the steady drip-dripping of the IV, laughter, the smell of french fries, ginger ale tabs fizz-popping open, texts pinging in from all directions.

"Are you doing okay?" I ask myself in the chemo bay.

"I think so," I say.

9. Suspicious Country

Right after the diagnosis, I find it nearly impossible to read. I can't think clearly, and I don't have the patience for the development of other people's ideas and images.

"Yeah, I had that, too," my mom says when I mention it to her. "I did a lot of staring at the wall. And I watched every single episode of *NCIS*. It's kind of like having a baby. Don't worry—you'll get back to it."

I remember a Christmas several years back when she was feeling very ill and directionless, and we spent a chilly weekend at the beach reading and discussing a biography of Michel de Montaigne. It left her on more solid ground. I pull out my old graduate school copy of the Montaigne *Essays* and start to read.

In one of my favorite essays he writes about his brother's sudden death at age twenty-three after being hit in the head by a tennis ball:

He did not sit down or rest, but five or six hours later he died of apoplexy caused by the blow.

With such frequent, common examples passing before our eyes, how can we possibly get rid of the thought of death; how can it not seem at every moment to be gripping us by the throat?

Montaigne came to know death well during his life in sixteenth-century France: the loss of five of his six daughters in childhood, the sudden demise of his closest friend in his arms at the hands of the plague, a lifetime of debilitating kidney stone attacks.

It is a continual source of torment that cannot be assuaged at all. There is no place from which it may not come; we may keep turning our heads ceaselessly this way and that, as in suspicious country.

Suspicious country—I'm beginning to know that place.

Certainly, it is the far better name for a boutique in town called A Special Place Wigs: a chemo/hair loss specialty shop full of hats, bright scarves, wigs, appeasing creams, even sad little yellowing packets of eyebrow pairs shaped of human hair.

The first time I went there, I opened the door gripping a paper prescription from my oncologist that said "head prosthesis." In my postdiagnosis haze, I had thrown out the first one she gave me, thinking: *Oh, this must be for someone else. I haven't lost my head.*

Katrine, the stylist, shaved off what was left of my hair in a back room and helped fit me for my wig. Tita took lots of pictures and we laughed and laughed.

Montaigne writes: "When a horse stumbles, a roof tile falls, however slightly a pin pricks, let us immediately ruminate on this: 'So, what if this were death itself?'"

When the scissors's snips are brusque and sudden. When the clippers buzz on. When your new hair emerges sleek and orderly from a shoebox.

I love about Montaigne that, despite roving bands of thieves and constant political upheaval, he reportedly never kept his castle guarded. He left all his doors unlocked. He acknowledged the terror that could come. But by considering it and allowing it in, he resolved to live with its presence: "I want death to find me planting my cabbages, not concerned about *it* or—still less—my unfinished garden."

My wig smells toxic and makes me feel like a bank robber. But maybe it is just a cloak for riding out into suspicious country.

10. I Believe (When I Fall in Love It Will Be Forever)

Freddy is eager to go back to school the day after he is released from the hospital. We show up in the nurse's office with meters and insulin pens and alcohol swabs and glucagon kits and care plans. He is mostly focused on the silver lining that now he is allowed to eat a seemingly unlimited amount of beef jerky. But I see him moving differently through the world now—like he always has a bag over his shoulder. A bag filled with the words: *Injections. Chronic disease. Glycemic index. Ketones. Hospital.*

Then I remember this one night in the early 1980s. My dad and I were riding in his old white pickup down Route 128 somewhere north of Boston when it overheated, leaving us stranded on the side of the highway in a thunderstorm.

This was the era when breaking down still meant walking to find a phone. And I was about eight—not really old enough to be left in a truck at night on the side of the highway. So, during a pause in the downpour the two of us set off into the long wet grass toward a smattering of dark houses not far from the exit ramp.

Everyone's power was out with the storm, and it took a few tries before we found someone with a working phone to let us call my mom, who was certainly starting to worry. Then we trekked back out to the truck to wait until she came to pick us up.

The truck battery was still working, so we cranked up my dad's favorite cassette at the time—Stevie Wonder's *Talking Book*. The windows were all fogged up and I still remember how the cab of that pickup smelled—a mix of sawdust and orange peels and dirt and coffee. Just like my dad.

I dozed a little in and out, my head lolling on the scratchy woven upholstery, with Stevie singing "I Believe (When I Fall in Love It Will Be Forever)" over and over again, and then we'd rewind and listen to it again and my dad would get kind of falsetto and harmonize-y on the "I Believe" part and I was the most contented, up-past-my-bedtime, headlights-in-the-dark-counting, adventure-haver there ever was. And then my mom arrived in our little Volkswagen Rabbit and ferried us home safely to bed.

Freddy is about the same age now as I was then. I'm trying to be wide open with him about his disease, my cancer, the treatment, the parts I'm nervous about—to make it less scary. Maybe not the capital *F* fears, but all the lower-case ones for sure.

I scan him for signs of trauma, distress, anger. I ask him how he's feeling about a hundred times a day, fending off my own topsy-turvy guilt and uncertainty.

The other day, poking at the latest IV scab on my hand, he said, "Sometimes I miss the hospital so much I could cry."

The hospital. The beeping machines. The sallow 3 a.m. light of the hallway. The narrow vinyl couch and paper sheet. My matted hair. My jumbled belongings on the chair, the pink breast cancer tote. The pee jug I nervously watched for signs of ketones in Freddy's urine. My son tangled in his tubes and wires. The four hours and twelve minutes when they thought he also had an undiagnosed heart problem. The endless parade of techs and nurses and doctors. *That* hospital?

"I loved playing those video games the whole time," he said. "And remember how you would climb in the bed and cuddle me at night and we would just talk?"

Oh. *That* hospital. The smell of his sweaty curls tucked under my chin. The way he would squeeze my hand whenever someone new walked into the room. The steady puffs of his breathing I hadn't lain awake listening to since he was a baby and I was a delirious new mother.

So here is the thing: Is it possible then that my dad wasn't actually having the time of his life like I was—after driving late at night in the rain, dragging his kid to strangers' houses, and sitting on the busy shoulder of Route 128 and eventually having to abandon his blown-up truck for the night?

That instead he was worried and exhausted and barely coping? Does "I Believe" conceivably not evoke a shimmery world of adventure for him? Does he not now sing it to himself alone in the car and every time feel happy and loved and excited about whatever might happen next?

A while ago, I asked him if he remembered that trip. "Oh, for sure. I was so wiped out when we got home."

I burned him a CD of *Talking Book* to replace his long-ago-busted cassette. The other night he had it on in the kitchen at his house, and it turns out thirty years later he still sings along in the exact same croony way to "I Believe."

Which makes my thinking go like this: When you fall in love with your kids, you fall in love forever. And that love forms the exact shape in the world of the cab of a beat-up pickup on the side of the dark highway—filled with safety and Stevie Wonder and okay-ness.

Or the exact shape of a single hospital bed with two figures nestled in it. Which of course suggests that no matter what, the kid is going to be all right.

11. Dancing with Myself

Before every chemo appointment Tita and her husband, Drew, text me selfies of themselves making crazy snarl-lipped pirate/Billy Idol–type faces. "Rock n roll, baby," Tita writes. "You've got this."

One time I am standing in the middle of the exam room trying to hold my blue hospital gown on while taking a selfie to send back to them of me making the same face when a tech opens the door without knocking. "Whoa. Everything okay in here, Ms. Riggs? You look a little off."

"I'm completely fine," I say, trying not to laugh. "I was just trying to pretend I was a rock star for my friend."

"Oh, okay," says the tech. "Well, I'll be right back with the nurse just in case. Please take a seat and press the blue button if you need anything."

12. The Poetry Fox

This one day at Duke, John and I spot a man in a furry fox suit. He's sitting in the lobby with a typewriter. You give him a word, and he furiously types up a poem based on it, as you wait.

I have a long wait at the crowded breast clinic, and John wanders off to find lunch. He stops by the poetry fox on the way back.

A woman ahead of him gets a rambling prose poem about a childhood memory of Poetry Fox's. Someone else gets a limerick composed around the word *hope*: *nope, soap, dope*. The fox seems a little worn down. When it is his turn, John gives the fox the word *nonplussed*.

"Nonplussed," says the fox. "Okay, fine." And he types out a free-verse poem that, while indicating that Poetry Fox also does not know the true dictionary meaning of *nonplussed*, is a worthy souvenir.

Stay / nonplussed. Make / them work / to crack / you, writes Poetry Fox, among other things.

"You'll like this," says John when he shows back up in the breast clinic with the typed poem.

"Hmm. That's not really my emotional philosophy," I say. "I like being cracked open."

"It's not a bad mantra for the medical journey, though," says John. "Especially considering it came from a man in a fox suit."

"Good point," I say. All the warfare jargon around cancer—the battling, the surviving, the winning/losing, the kicking its ass—hasn't been ringing true for me. But I'm good with not letting it crack me.

"I will be the densest little nut in the world," I say to John. "Green and unyielding. A squirrel's effing nightmare."

"One small spot," says John, squeezing my hand.

13. Dasein

John and I met in a graveyard. It was during college at a summer job in Carlisle, Pennsylvania, where we were both teaching assistants at a camp for gifted kids. I taught a writing class and he taught a course on existentialism. Our classes would sometimes cross paths on field trips to the historic, treeless cemetery down the street from the campus where the camp was held. Overlapping interests, you could say.

"How's your class going?" John asks as we both wander around the graveyard distributing handouts. He's got these crazy blue eyes and a backward ball cap and a sexy smile, and he's wearing a Bad Religion T-shirt and carrying a dog-eared copy of Sartre's *Being and Nothingness*—in French. I mean: Forget it.

"Not bad," I say. "I'll be relieved when the session is over though. Sounding like I know what I'm talking about all day is kind of beyond me. These kids are really smart."

"Yeah. Try adding Kant to that," he says.

"I kant," I manage.

I tell him I'm so tired I keep saying "kill-dren" by mistake when I mean to say *children*.

"You'll make a fantastic mother someday," he says.

Journal prompts for the graveyard: *Steal a name and dates off a headstone and write a character sketch. Describe something you see here without revealing the setting. Imagine and describe your own death. Write the first paragraph of a love story that begins in this cemetery.*

John's students read Kierkegaard and stare off into hand mirrors they've brought as props near my students. The grass in the graveyard is so sharp and dry and full of anthills you can hardly sit down, and there is never a single bit of wind to rile the rows of veteran flags. If there is any sound at all other than the occasional muscle car revving through the stoplight at the corner, it is the sound of bees. Big loud desperate bees and the quieter, tiny, metallic-looking bees that cluster at your ankles. Sweat bees, those little ones are called.

One day, three girls from my class come find me at the oversize cement skirts and raised ramrod of the Molly Pitcher monument near the entrance gate and tell me that a man had just appeared near where they were sitting and loaded a trap with a groundhog inside into his pickup. They say the groundhog was jumping all around in the trap and the man whacked it over the head with a shovel until it stopped moving. One of the girls is crying.

"Yikes," I say. "But I guess now you have an amazing plot twist for your story." They shrug and walk away. I decide it's probably time to head back to the classroom.

"See you at the dining hall," I say to John with a meaningful stare, "if in fact you exist." He rolls his eyes and goes back to explaining Heidegger's *Dasein* to a thirteen-year-old with purple hair and wool hand-knit shorts.

*   *   *

I've always loved Molly Pitcher, that Revolutionary War super-mom who traipsed into battle fearlessly stirring pots, tending wounds, scrubbing bloodstains, in all the fourth-grade history books.

She's the one who found a hidden spring during a one-hundred-degree day of gun fighting at Monmouth and brought cold, fresh water to the soldiers. And then later that afternoon it is said that she picked up her husband's rammer after he dropped from exhaustion at his cannon and set to work swabbing and loading and blasting the British back to Sandy Hook, New Jersey.

Also: There was the time when the skirt was ripped from her frock by a British musket ball that passed between her legs, and Molly supposedly exclaimed, *"Well, that could have been worse!"*

I think about Molly Pitcher all the time these days—whenever I feel like I'm standing in a battlefield with my heart pounding and a gaping hole burned out of my dress.

When my pubic hair all falls out at once in the shower and shows up like a drowned baby muskrat in the drain. When I'm summoned to the elementary school to discuss some unfortunate behavior on the part of my elder son, and a kindergartener in the hall sees me and starts to cry. When I try to dye Easter eggs with the kids and end up gagging over the smell of sulfur and vinegar in the bathroom. When I wake one morning covered in hives, my lips and eyes swollen like I was nearly punched to death.

My friend Melissa, who is the closest real-life person I know to

Molly Pitcher, picks my kids up from school, keeps them for hours while simultaneously running her own business, and organizes a parade of friends who show up on our stoop with dinner night after night: soups and roast chickens and eggplant parmesans. At first I try to look human when people stop by, but eventually I stop. Cancer removes whatever weird barriers we sometimes have with others. A *mastectomy of bullshit,* my mother suggests. All the oh-yes-everything-is-great stuff eventually gets carted off in a bag of medical waste.

One morning with my class in the Carlisle graveyard, I found a headstone near Molly Pitcher for someone named Molly McCauley. I looked it up in the local library later and it turned out she was the actual woman: a well-liked servant for hire—known for cursing like a soldier—who lived and died in Carlisle. And that Molly Pitcher is made-up—probably a legend from centuries of lore or maybe some tall tale the author of all fourth-grade textbooks made up when his wife asked him to help fold the laundry.

I ended up feeling kind of annoyed at the myth on behalf of Real Molly—and became increasingly fond of her lesser-known story of hard work and quiet survival with the help of a few curse words.

And I got fonder of the sweat bees, too—even though they stung me a couple times. They like sweaty, sweet, humans for goodness sake. Don't we all: John and I got married exactly two years later.

I love the gutsy cement hero woman and I also love the real

potty-mouthed housemaid with a ruffled bonnet who is buried somewhere below that crooked, faceless grave. I love the musket ball not hitting me, and I also love the musket ball. I love *goddammit motherfucker*, and I really love *Well, that could have been worse.*

14. The Transparent Eyeball

Steroids: I wake up with the oily taste of chemo in my mouth—even the flavor of coffee slides off my tongue. I don't belong in bed, but I don't fit in out in the world either. I have a sense of myself as a broken camera—focusing on something out on the horizon (the future, cure, recurrence, death) and then, without warning, zooming in on a blade of grass (*what is that weird taste in my mouth, is that a new lump, thank you for this beautiful card, this beautiful meal, did anyone remember to pack a snack for the kids*). And then zooming out to the horizon again, and then back, and then again. I can't figure out where I'm supposed to point this thing.

I know I can't sit inside for one more minute so I head for the woods, where today it is so brutally green and alive it almost hurts, and I feel I am being drugged with the scent of wisteria. At first I am nearly running—I cannot slow my body—and I can feel in my chest and my fingertips the thrum of some electric-like current and my heartbeat in my ears. But then my breathing takes over and I start to slow down—and that steadying step pulses in the leaves and roots and through the moss that lines the forest floor.

There is a striking sketch from the late 1830s by transcendentalist artist and writer Christopher Pearse Cranch that was made to illustrate the concept of the "transparent eye-ball" in Ralph Waldo Emerson's essay *Nature*. Emerson felt that nature was the closest we can get to experiencing God, and he believed that in order to truly appreciate nature, you must not only look at it and admire it, but also be able to feel it taking over the senses. The transparent eyeball absorbs—rather than reflects—what it perceives:

> Standing on the bare ground,—my head bathed by the blithe air, and uplifted into infinite spaces,—all mean egotism vanishes. I become a transparent eye-ball; I am nothing; I see all; the currents of the Universal Being circulate through me; I am part or particle of God.

In the Cranch illustration, a giant eyeball on long, gangly legs and bare feet stands in an open meadow with hills on the horizon. The eyeball wears a top hat and an Emersonian waistcoat. It's a funny and beautiful image, and it is exactly how the drugs make me feel: I am a ludicrous eyeball: I edit nothing out: All currents circulate through me and I take them all in. Emerson rolling in his grave: Steroids and chemo are the closest I get to God.

One afternoon my dad stops by on the way home from work to tell me he heard on the radio that all humans have a physiological blind spot located about twelve to fifteen inches out from our faces. My dad, a retired builder, now works as a handyman at several apartment complexes in town. He wears a pager and gets beeped at all hours of the day and night to replace a kicked-in door, reseat a toilet, refloor a flooded kitchen, rekey a lock. He doesn't mind it at all. In fact, I think he loves it. He hates sitting still, and in this job he gets to zip around town in his minivan listening to NPR and dash in and out of hardware stores and people's lives.

"I'm hardly ever bored," he says. "And I get to hang out mostly in my own world—and that's where I make the most sense."

He's known for being a little spaced-out and sometimes saying off-the-wall things. There was this famous time in my early twenties when my mom and John and I all smoked a joint together before going out to dinner at a fancy restaurant, and my dad—who smoked one joint too many in the '60s and '70s—abstained. We all agreed he had never seemed more lucid or made more sense.

About the blind spot: He tells me that apparently it is the place in the visual field where the optic nerve passes through the optic disc, right where all the light-receptor cells are located. We rarely notice it because our other eye can often see what is happening, and if not—if the blind spots overlap—our brain does the work of filling in the missing information.

"Kinda cool, huh?" he says. "Interesting metaphor. We're perfectly imperfect designs."

Cool—unless all you are is one single giant eyeball. The blind spot stretches and grows.

We look it up on my laptop and find an online test that simulates the blind spot—a plus sign and a circle next to each other on a white screen. Sure enough, the circle completely disappears when you shut one of your eyes and hold the screen about a foot away.

"I wonder how big the blind spot could be, hypothetically, before your brain wouldn't be able to compensate accurately," I say.

"I like the idea that it's inaccurate at any size," says my dad. "One little spot of guesswork everywhere you look."

On chemo, I'd like to crawl inside that blind spot, whatever its size—scrunch up my body and disappear. *That,* the brain imagines, *is a drop of rain on a windshield, the abdomen of a bee, a tanager on a high branch, a crescent of moon—no—wait—a full moon.*

The thing with blind spots: you never see them coming. The night my dad graduated from high school he was in a head-on accident with a car he never saw. When his vision was later checked, they discovered he was nearly blind. Youngest of six kids: high-powered often-absent father, self-reliant mother with aristocratic New England breeding who did not do anything she was not called to do—and preferred taming horses to taming children, and a family with too much of a Puritan edge to consider employing help. He ran wild and mostly below the radar—never had his eyes checked, his learning difficulties diagnosed, or was taken to a lesson in anything. His parents didn't even give him a middle name.

"I was amazed to discover that tree branches were full of individual leaves and that brick walls were an arrangement of hundreds of separate red stones," he remembers. "I had never considered the idea of grout. After the accident, when I first got my glasses, I walked around in a state of constant disbelief."

Somehow he survived. Somehow he grew up into the most competent person I know. He can: ride a horse, head a soccer ball, fry a chicken, fix a washing machine, fix an engine, tether a boat in a storm, dance the foxtrot, build a tree house, work out a tune on the piano, calm a baby, win at rummy. He never complains about anything, even though in my lifetime so far he's been struck by lightning, been bitten by a brown recluse, and lost his life partner.

My parents met in San Francisco in the early 1970s. My mom was living in the Haight, recovering from her first marriage, which had ended when she came home early one day to discover her husband in his underwear in the living room with another man.

"And amazingly it almost didn't end then," my mom told me once. "I almost said, 'Oh, that's okay.' That's how naïve I was. He had to sort of prompt me through the breakup."

At eighteen, she had moved to San Francisco—the city where her mother grew up—from her home in the very sheltered Panama Canal Zone, where she'd lived as the daughter of an angry, domineering boat captain and deeply depressed nurse. She found rebellion, close friends, a good job as a medical transcriptionist—and eventually my dad, who was working at the time for a Fred Astaire dance studio and who recruited his real estate agent and my mom—her roommate—to help him get an extra twenty dollars that the studio paid for bringing in new clients.

They had a quick and rocky romance: my dad goofy and kind-hearted and young, rebelling against the war and his overbearing Yankee family, my mom a little more mature and already tortured by her uncertainty around the role she was supposed to play in the world.

"The first night I spent with him I woke up to a car honking outside at dawn," she often remembered. "He leapt up from bed and threw two pairs of underwear and a toothbrush into a paper bag and told me he was going rafting in Colorado and would be back in a week. I should have got up out of that bed and walked away right then."

She didn't. They got married at City Hall. They had a ball together and also fought about the meaning of "getting your life together." I was born in 1977. In 1982, my dad working construction and my mom still typing, they came to a tenuous agreement about what that might be, and one day we hopped in our Volkswagen Rabbit with a little trailer pulling behind and drove East—to Concord, back into the arms of the family my dad had left behind fifteen years earlier. We were offered a little cottage on my great-grandparents' estate to set up a home.

My great-grandparents on my dad's side are Emersons, and RWE is my great-great-great grandfather. Speaking of Molly Pitcher's legendary cement skirts, descending from someone who casts a shadow isn't simple work. Like many members of my extended family, I am still searching for the edge of the shadow that Emerson casts: He draws me to him, he pushes me away. Particularly that American monolith *Self-Reliance*: "Trust thyself: every heart vibrates to that iron string." Close one eye, the iconic essay is a handbook for geniuses and a rallying cry for quirky individualism. Close the other eye, and it's a recipe for indulgent self-obsession and a parenting nightmare: "What I must do is all that concerns me, not what the people think."

The people: That's what Freddy calls us when he's not happy with us. "Benny, the people say we can't watch any TV tonight." They are Emerson's descendants, too—another kind of blind spot altogether.

Emerson tracks me down anyway—another round of chemo, another tromp in the woods. *One small spot* I chant, giant eyeball crunching down the path, as though repeating the little phrase will keep me better attached to the spinning planet. But also I think of what the great man wrote in my favorite of his essays, *Circles*: "The universe is fluid and volatile." I've been rereading. "Permanence is but a word of degrees."

I try to hold both of these ideas like two little magnets in my hand: his and mine. *One small spot* and *the universe is fluid and volatile*. They push against each other: "One small spot" requires the constant energy to keep things contained. The "universe is fluid and volatile" is scary, but allows for the idea that there are things that cannot be contained. These two thoughts flip around and now cannot be pulled apart.

Thirty-three years ago: I am five years old, standing on a hillside with my cousins. It is the centenary of Emerson's death, and we are all holding a giant wreath at his grave site. We are his great-great-great grandchildren. A reporter takes our picture. I remember the weight of the giant wreath and the nip of Massachusetts spring on my bare legs where I had refused to wear tights.

"The eye is the first circle; the horizon which it forms is the second," he says at the opening of that essay. Circles—like cells, like planets, like families, like the spots of light that dance in your eyelashes at morning's first opening. He writes:

> Our life is an apprenticeship to the truth, that around every circle another can be drawn; that there is no end in nature, but every end is a beginning; that there is always another dawn risen on mid-noon, and under every deep a lower deep opens.

Here is the small spot; here the densest nut. Here is the musket ball hole. Here is the shape in the world of your child, you wrapped around your child. Here is the dark pool in the thickest woods. Here is the sun that sets in your eyes.

Thirty-three years ago: My mother is frowning. *You should have worn tights.* I am running with my cousins in the graveyard after the ceremony. "Come here," someone whispers. It is my cousin Bonnie, who is also five. She has found a hiding spot for us. We are behind a gravestone. "Everyone will find us here, and then we will all laugh so hard," she says—the best idea I have ever heard.

15. Shave

When the hair falls out, it is patchy and not vaguely pretty.

"This isn't working for you, is it?" says Tita. "I think we need to give you a nice badass Sinéad O'Connor vibe."

John performs my first official shave with his electric clippers on the front porch where I used to give the boys their trims. "Lift your chin really high and try not to breathe deep or anything."

"No problem," I say. "I haven't had a deep breath in years."

16. Empty Ocean

At chemo, they can never find my veins anymore. It's a side effect of the chemo itself, which has a way of frying whatever it touches. Dr. Cavanaugh is resistant to my getting a port put in: "I don't want anything unnecessary messing with your immune system at this point."

"It's like I'm fishing in a big, empty ocean," says one of the nurses, examining my arm with one of their high-tech vein-finders as I stare out the window. "It's pretty lonely in there. I'm so sorry I can't find anything."

Just outside the treatment area is a roof deck with picnic tables and lounge chairs and huge planters full of flowers. A family is unpacking bags and bags of Chick fil-A.

"Once we get the drugs going can I take my IV and go sit out there?" I ask the nurse. "I think the sun would feel good."

It's always chilly in the cancer center, and early on you learn to never say no to the warmed blankets they offer you. They might be the very best thing about the place.

"No," she says. "Sorry. Patients aren't allowed out there. Just family members. Isn't that ridiculous?"

One of the children with the picnicking family is breaking off pieces of waffle fry and tossing them over the railing. The mother is holding him on her lap, but hasn't noticed. She is talking urgently on the phone and keeps glancing back in at all of us patients in the treatment area. A grandmother looks on from across the table, smiling and clapping with the child each time a chunk of food disappears over the rail. At chemo, I can never find my center anymore. It's like a big, empty ocean.

17. Fire Alarm

"What do they do to you at chemo?" asks Benny as I'm snuggling in bed with the boys before school. Every morning while John is in the shower, they both run from their room and climb in here and we power cuddle. Freddy has me draw pictures with my fingers on his back that he has to identify. Benny behaves like some kind of baby animal that I have to guess each morning.

This morning, he keeps sniffing and scrunching his nose and wagging his bottom and making little yipping noises. "A baby fennec fox," I say. "Nice, Mom!" he exclaims.

Don't get too excited: I have an inside line. He's been a fennec fox the last six days in a row.

"So, they put me in a chair and they give me medicine," I tell them, sketching my fingers over Freddy's back. "It's actually not too bad."

Both of the boys dislike chemo days because when they leave me I'm pretty normal and can help them fix their waffles and everything, and by the time they get home from school I'm pale and cranky and want to be left alone.

"I would escape," says Freddy. "I would get Benny to pull the fire alarm and then I would run out the door when no one was paying attention."

"But I want the medicine," I say. "Just like when you were in the hospital and we wanted the medicine to help with your diabetes."

"Oh man. I always forget that part," says Freddy. I've just finished sketching a hot air balloon on his back. "Is it a heart? I mean, not a heart symbol but like a real human heart with veins coming out of it?"

"No. But I like yours better," I say, erasing the smooth skin slate with the pads of my fingers.

18. Advanced Directive

More suspicious country: What would Montaigne make of signing a will or an advanced directive or a health-care power of attorney— of the notaries and their poised stamps and the smell of coffee brewing; the documents and their copies of copies of copies; the fresh black ballpoints scattered on the board room table?

John and I take the elevator to the nineteenth floor of the building where John used to work in private practice. I have worn a sundress but I am suddenly very cold and longing for a sweater. Our friend, Adam—an expert in handling estates with dozens more zeros than ours—works at the firm and is standing there to greet us when the doors open.

Adam and his wife, Melissa, are close enough friends of ours that we have considered them possible guardians of our children. Their kids are our kids' best friends. I went to grad school with both Adam and Melissa; John and Adam later survived law school together; our four boys were all born at the same time; we live around the corner from each other. We vacation together, spend Saturday evenings cooking in each other's kitchens, hug and feed and reprimand each other's kids as if they were our own.

"Ugh," says Adam when he sees us. "Hi. Sorry you have to be here."

"If they're lucky and smart, everyone ends up here eventually," says John.

Adam's assistant is printing endless stacks of papers and we swivel in the cushy office chairs as she finishes. "Can I get you all a Diet Coke or anything?" she asks. We do not need a thing.

"So, do people actually ever do really insane things in their wills," I ask Adam as we wait for everything to be collated, "like give their estates to their dog or a waitress at the coffee shop or bury it on a desert island or whatever?"

"Yup," he says, and not one more word. Adam knows all the best secrets in town and wouldn't tell a single one if his life depended on it, even when he's had a lot to drink.

Both Adam and Melissa are trained as poets, but I question Adam's instincts as a fiction writer.

"I don't love all the drama in my job," he told me once at a party. "The feuds and the illegitimate kids and the spurned ex-wives and the twenty-year-olds that suddenly stand to inherit millions of dollars. I try to just block it out."

"Are you crazy?" I said. "I would be taking detailed notes. I would be entertaining Melissa all evening. I would be making millions of my own dollars writing shelves and shelves of the most juicy, sordid best sellers ever."

"Yeah, I'm thinking you might not make it as a lawyer for very long," he said.

Perusing the documents, Adam has to direct us to some tough questions before we can sign: the world's darkest quantitative reasoning test. "Check next to your preferred option," he says.

I want to receive BOTH artificial hydration AND artificial nu-

trition. *I want to receive ONLY artificial hydration AND NOT artificial nutrition (for example, through tubes). I want to receive ONLY artificial nutrition AND NOT artificial hydration (for example, through tubes). I want to receive NEITHER artificial hydration NOR artificial nutrition.*

Then: "Initial here if you prefer SHALL. Or here if you prefer MAY," he says in his calm voice, just like: *Do you all want wine or a beer?*

In the case that I am incapacitated, my health-care providers MAY withhold or withdraw life-prolonging measures or SHALL withhold or withdraw life-prolonging measures.

I look at John and kind of shrug and initial next to *SHALL.* May or shall. I may go for a stroll on the moors later. I shall be late for tea.

But of course: no. That is not it at all.

"Why does our common language, which is so plain in its other uses, become obscure and unintelligible in contracts and wills?" asks Montaigne.

I have an inkling. I'm sure Montaigne did, too, if he lingered at all on that thought—the tennis ball careening through the cool morning, our heads turning ceaselessly this way and that. It is exactly like the immaculate conference room, the stacks of papers, the brewing coffee, the notary and witnesses in waiting, Adam in his tie.

I, NINA ELLEN RIGGS, the Testator, sign my name to this instrument, and being first duly sworn, do hereby declare to the undersigned authority that I sign and execute this instrument as my Last Will and Testament and that I sign it willingly, that I execute it as my free and voluntary act for the purposes therein expressed, and that I am eighteen years of age or older, of sound mind, and under no constraint or undue influence.

Here is what it says eight hours later in our plain and common language—kitchen darkened, kids asleep. It takes all its clothes off next to the bed. It searches the hook for the nightgown, massages the lump that presses against the skin at just past midnight on the breast clock, glances at itself in the mirror. *I am gone.* It says: *I was here—right here—look at this ink, the curl of the N—and now I am gone, and I leave these things to you: my spouse, JOHN A. DUBER-STEIN, because you have survived me.*

19. In the Dark

A warm evening. Dinner party on the back deck—candles, another good bottle brought to the cleared table, a swarm of children darting in the backyard.

We piece it together later—long after the dishes are dried and John is tugging off my shirt and Freddy shows up in our doorway saying there is something "very Scooby Doo" happening over his bed and I watch a bat swoop out from the boys' room into the stairwell—that the screen door must have been left partly open.

But my feeling was that the bat *had* to be mad to enter during the evening's buggiest hours—inching along the molding and flattening in the curtain folds and making its way upstairs.

An aimless chase, and we corner it in the mudroom, but then it disappears into the infinite nowhere of our clutter—immortal just like that—possible in every deep cupboard, every stack of towels, every tool bag.

For hours John and I stand shifts in the darkening and darkened yard. I hold the rake for courage and watch the lit mudroom for any flutter, any fleck of brown, any glimmer of certainty to confirm: location, manner, existence.

The loud dark lawn is an unsettled audience—crickets and cicadas, their restless catcalls. Night is a belly of bugs, and all around, other bats were leaving their roosts in trees and chimneys, signaling flight with ultrasonic clicks, a neutral, hollow sound—

surprisingly unmammalian—the sound of thought, the sound that asks you not to pull apart the pieces of night:

A snake's rattle, but much slower, the freewheel on a bicycle coasting downhill, an invisible child dragging a stick along a fence, the lullaby I concocted for Benny as a baby on those million nights of his waking—

the flag says thwap thwap thwap,
the fan says clickity clack,
the lights go blinkity blinkity blinkity
blinkity blinkity black.

It was a song I never sang very gently, but with a kind of conviction.

20. More Steroids

I have wallpapered the mudroom and reorganized the tools and the pegboard. I have installed a pea-gravel patio and a fire pit in the backyard next to the new deck my dad built for us. I have planted herbs, annuals, peppers, and squash. Three new hydrangeas, a gardenia, a Japanese maple. A trellis, a climbing clematis, a little shade garden near the willow oak. Boxes of geraniums. I have assembled a rocking chair and spread fifteen bags of mulch. I only stop planting because I'm avoiding the cashier at the garden center. "Welcome back again, Nina," he says when I walk in through the gate. He knows my name from my debit card. I know his from his name tag. "Hi, Clark," I say without being able to make eye contact.

Every day when John comes home from work I drag him out to the yard and beam expectantly. "Please stop," he says. "It's beautiful, but you have to slow down."

"Make me," I say. Tears explode from my eyes.

"Have you tried actually sitting in the rocking chair yet?" he asks, hugging me.

Then I'm up late reading Montaigne essays and dozens of articles about gardening that I find on Pinterest. And I'm up late reading cancer books: *Radical Remission: Surviving Cancer Against All Odds*; Paul Kalanithi's gorgeous memoir; Claudia Emerson's brutal book of poems, *Late Wife*. And I'm reading

Svetlana Alexievich's *Voices from Chernobyl* because I can't stop reading it—even though my book club rejected it for being too dark. Instead, we settle on Adam Johnson's bone-chilling novel about life in North Korea, *The Orphan Master's Son*, so I'm up late reading that, too.

21. Book Club

For years, my mom has hosted book club at her house every month. She likes not having to go out. It's her and three of her close friends: Linda, Anne, and Teresa. And me and Tita. My mom always sits in the giant leather chair in the living room and doesn't eat very much. The drug from the clinical trial she is on makes her feel nauseated a lot of the time—although she is almost always dressed and mostly cheerful and up for a glass or two of wine. The rest of us gather around on the sectional, eating smoked salmon on crackers and salad.

"It's a good thing that we read *Orphan Master's Son* instead of something dark," jokes Tita. "Isn't there a book version of *Schindler's List* we could try next?"

"Oh come on," says my mom. "Why is everyone so afraid of the dark?" She's only half kidding.

"Maybe we're not," I say. "Maybe we just feel like we're supposed to be." But I can tell that not everyone agrees with me.

"It seems like our most fun discussions happen when we get to trash the really terrible, shallow books," says Linda.

"True," says Anne, whose taste runs very similar to mine. "The beautiful, heavy ones have a way of shutting us all up. But I think somehow I'm okay with that."

"Me too," says Teresa, who loves heavy-duty historical non-fiction.

"I don't know," says Linda. "I guess I'm open to the dark stuff—I can always skim. But I can't deal with cruelty to animals. No tortured dogs or horses or anything. That's where I draw the line."

"Totally agree," says Tita. We all end up nodding.

"Are we weird or what?" says my mom. "Tortured men, raped teenagers, dying mothers: We'll somehow endure those. But skeletal dogs: No way, José."

We settle on *Factory Man*, a book about the decline of the furniture industry in southern Virginia, for next month.

22. Beastie Cats

Two nights before my postchemo scan I have a dream so imposing it displaces my reality for most of the following day.

I'm lying in a darkened ultrasound room, gooped up with ultrasound goop, my right side propped on the foam wedge, arm curled above my head, and the doctor is running the transducer across my chest and into my armpit like a little boy zooming his matchbox car. I look up at the screen where usually all you see is that strange universe of shadows and ghosts that is allegedly your insides, and instead I see two tigers pacing the perimeter of my chest wall.

It's not a totally foreign image. We have two tigers of our own in Greensboro. Two startling four-hundred-pounders, part Bengal, part Siberian, rescued from somewhere—maybe the offspring of circus tigers—that live tucked in the woods that abut Lawndale Avenue at the Greensboro Science Center.

Beastie cats, one of the boys used to call them.

There are a number of fascinating but unnerving things about the tigers: the way they hyperfixate on stroller wheels and errant toddlers; the volume at which they both roar when the male mounts the female (not infrequently); how some suburban Greensboro subdivision practically backs up to their habitat, how the female keeps incessant watch from her rock lookout while the male naps in the shade, how in some spots there is basically just the equivalent of an elementary schoolyard baseball backstop between you and them.

But the most disconcerting thing about the beastie cats is how they pace. It's that measured, obsessive, nervous stalking you might recognize from your dog during a thunderstorm or a restless night before a set of important scans.

The science center keepers say the reason the tigers pace is because they are craving human contact—they were bottle-fed as babies, and they miss being close to people, which is why they like the perimeter of the enclosure so much. It's where the people are.

I don't know. What is this, really? It reads a little more like madness to me. Decades before she was diagnosed with breast cancer, the poet Jorie Graham wrote this about the hot, dry scirocco wind in Italy:

Who is

the nervous spirit
of this world
that must go over and over
what it already knows

Maybe it's not really madness though. Maybe it's an entirely sane response to being denied human contact. Or to very many things—results and treatment protocols and the future.

So, the beastie cats are pacing the chest wall.

Yesterday morning—after a restorative, humanizing walk in the near-rain among many heart-stoppingly beautiful blooming gardens and yards with a good friend who lost both her parents in a year and whose dog just died—I was remembering the dream. Simultaneously nonplussed and not nonplussed, I was thinking: *There are tigers in the woods here and they are a little off their rockers, but that's the place where we live.*

STAGE TWO

1. Something Gray Like Grief

First ultrasound ever: I'm sixteen weeks pregnant. The darkened room, John standing at my side. We're watching the tech—then a doctor who enters from another room, then another doctor—wade again and again into the ocean of my belly, find our growing boy there—his spine curving like driftwood, his thunderous heart. It's the strangest thing we've ever seen. We can't stop watching the screen/ocean. Him.

But they're taking too many pictures. Too many measurements. His feet. His legs. His brain. His heart. His feet again. No one is talking at all, until suddenly someone says, "Well, I guess by now you know something is not quite right."

We don't exactly, but we were starting to. We've never been here before. I find myself remembering the time we took our old dog, Zilch, to the ocean for the first time.

We let him out of the backseat of the car, and he beelined for the beach—racing circles in the dry sand, sniffing the bite of tidal decay, knots of seaweed, rotting crab shells, a dried black purse of skate eggs.

Eventually he nosed his way to low tide's edge, the gentle lick of the inlet slapping the sand, and then, when the wet of seawater meets the wet of nose, he froze, as though only just then realizing this was not his backyard water bowl.

We watched as he planted his front paws into the uncertain earth, then raised a wary head to scan his surroundings—where the ocean reached in a thousand blue directions, as massive and inscrutable as sleep, as bad news.

He took two steps backward, stopped, and growled. The world was even stranger than before. Something gray like grief passed through his eyes before he turned his glance to a low-flying gull and chased it.

Talipes equinovarus, they tell us after the scan—club foot. It sounds like something that has been flung toward us from the dark ages. My brain is groping through *Beowulf. Idiopathic,* they say. Sounds like Greek for a Shakespearean fool, but it turns out this is good news: not part of a larger, scarier complex of issues. Just the foot. The right foot.

Not the world ending, but the ground shifting. Everything is stranger than before. *Will he walk?* They are talking about surgeons and casting and braces, about cutting his Achilles tendon just after birth. We have only just learned he is a he. *Fixable,* they keep saying.

Later at home, John bans me from obsessing on the Internet, but agrees to read me a list of people he finds born with club feet. It turns out it's not just obscure, misanthropic rulers. There are athletes on the list: Troy Aikman. Kristi Yamaguchi. Mia Hamm. Freddy Sanchez—who won the batting title in 2006 for John's hometown team, the Pittsburgh Pirates, and for whom the shapes

in the ultrasound-verse will soon be named. Eight years later—
leg casts, orthotic brace, surgery—we watch him round the bases,
slide into third.

Today at the postchemo scan, I'm back on the table. It's a lot like
my dream, dim and goopy, so I tell the radiologist about the tigers.

"Hmmmm—two tigers, huh?" she says. She's measuring, she's
taking pictures—click clicking on the keyboard. Measuring again.
Too many pictures.

"Well, I can't say I love what I'm seeing," she eventually says.
Something gray like grief.

The tumor is still there. It is not smaller. In fact, it is bigger
than they first thought. It seems to reach in a thousand directions.
And, on top of that, there is another tumor a few centimeters away
that has surfaced from some depth previously unseeable. A second
tiger.

"We will need to do some more tests," she says.

The ground shifts—it just does. I text John in the waiting room
and know his footing is shifting, too. Things are stranger than before.

Zilch never really became an ocean dog. He was short, below
wave height—a beagle/corgi mix—and lower in the front than the
back. But later that same afternoon, for a moment, he did chase a
gull right out into the shallows and hardly even looked down.

2. Occult Tumor

The Duke Aesthetic Center, where my breast surgeon's office is housed, is brand-spanking new and very lovely—tucked back among perfectly perky B-cup-size rolling hills in a shaded medical park with two long-legged parking lots.

So fresh and Truman Show-ish is the whole complex, in fact, it almost seems fortunate that we arrive a little late to my appointment to give the numerous landscapers time to lay out more pine straw. I'm pretty sure a couple boxwoods are hastily planted as we walk down the pathway toward the office.

The waiting room is silent and comfortable. Two other women sit leafing through magazines, but they don't speak or look up or have their names called, and they look suspiciously like set extras.

Later the surgeon's nurse will tell me they are "fluff n' puffs." Boob jobs. They get seen after the cancer patients.

When the surgeon enters the exam room he says, "You've sure thrown us a curveball here, young lady." The new tumor is malignant, and surgeons love to blame the patient. "Now we're going to have to do a mastectomy instead of the lumpectomy. Up to you if you want to do a twofer on the mastectomy."

Montaigne summons Plato's belief that doctors should ideally experience all the illnesses they seek to cure: "It is right for them to catch the pox if they want to know how to treat it." He sounds a little cranky here, but he suffered through a number of kidney stones and I can imagine that might predispose you to crankiness.

I ask the surgeon if he would recommend a double mastectomy if it were his wife—the question you're always supposed to ask. He hedges.

"We're all different," he says. He tells us the tumors are shaped like a dumbbell, with each tumor being one of the weights on either end. And between them—no one's totally sure but—what looks to be a four-centimeter-long bar of cancerous material. He calls my new lump an *occult tumor*—hidden on earlier imaging.

It feels as though they might be really into drama over here at the Aesthetic Center.

"I definitely didn't expect this twist," he says gravely, but with a little excitement brimming in his voice.

I can't help but think about a surgeon who one of the chemo nurses once told me about. It was back in the 1970s and early '80s, when she worked in radiation oncology, and she used to see all the patient files. The doctor recommended a radical mastectomy—a disfiguring procedure where not only is all the breast tissue removed, but so is much of the underlying chest muscle—in 100 percent of his patients.

Although it had been standard practice for decades, the traumatic procedure fell out of favor in the mid-'70s due to improvements in our understanding of the spread of cancer cells. This surgeon, however, kept recommending radical mastectomies until the day his wife got breast cancer.

"Not for her," said the chemo nurse. "That was when he performed his first simple mastectomy."

As John and I leave the building, there are still no cars in the parking lot. And I can't make out the name of a single other practice in the complex—too dappled is the shade. I feel John's foot heavy on the pedal as we hurry from the driveway into the pristine cul-de-sac, not totally certain if we are escaping—or complicit in—some new, dark art.

3. Dispatch from the Dark

Speaking of the dark: It's past midnight, and we're lying in bed. "I just can't wait for things to get back to normal," says John from his side of the moon.

I'm not sure how to respond. I hadn't realized how attached I have become to the idea that, even in all of this, we are moving ahead somehow, and that dealing with all this is something to value. I feel a sharpness in my throat, the slip of the sureness beneath me.

"I can't handle you saying that," I say after a silence, even though I know he isn't trying to fight. "Thinking that way kind of invalidates my whole life right now. I have to love these days in the same way I love any other. There might not be a 'normal' from here on out."

He's not happy. I feel the cool bricks of an invisible wall settling into place between us. I turn away to face the window, a heavy orange haze filtering in through the trees. It's not as dark out as it should be.

"I don't believe you," he says. "I don't think you're being honest." It's the tone I've heard him use when I've told him I think he's being a shitty parent. Or that no matter what I'm probably never going to like watching hockey. Anger that morphs from hurt. "I really think you're in some kind of whacked-out denial right now if you think these days are loveable."

"These days are days," I say, calm and furious. "We choose how we hold them. Good night."

Around 4 a.m. I feel his hand on my back. "I'm so afraid I can't breathe," he whispers.

"I know," I say, scootching a little toward him but still facing away. "So am I."

Montaigne: "I learn to mistrust my steps everywhere, and I take care to control them."

He also believes in lively shouting matches before meals and only "begetting children" before sleep. We are doing it all wrong.

4. Say Please

My kids think I'm obsessed with the word *please.*

Why is it so important, they whine, *what's the big deal?* I make them a list one night. A list they won't possibly understand for twenty to thirty years, but I am trying to write things down:

Because you will find that the fruit will drop, but rarely into your mouth.

Because the bathroom faucet sticks, and *please* makes the stronger hand less weary.

Because on summer nights the expectant sky cloaks the trees like a bed sheet, and storm cells spit tornados toward us from deeper south, and the willow oak in the backyard is a monster, and every night we lie down at its feet. Because we never taught you to pray.

Because at night you are thirsty.

Because someday your children, on the other side of your wall, will cackle into the darkness long past their bedtime.

Because right now through the open windows I can hear the newlyweds next door carving out a backyard patio by lamplight, deliberating as they kneel together in their yard, placing flagstones. The stones they hand each other are heavy and oddly shaped. And they must level each one in the dirt—tapping, cajoling, and swaddling the difficult rocks—and then make their way upstairs to bed.

Because the *s* in please is the sweetest sound, like steam rising after a summer shower, like a baby whispering in his bed.

Because you are human, and it is your nature to ask for more.

Because *want, need*—those unlit cul-de-sacs—are too perilous unadorned.

5. Mother and Daughter Tour Italy

I opt for a single mastectomy at Dr. Cavanaugh's urging. *Halves the chance of complications*, she says. Halving, dividing, splitting, cutting—this is our new language: cells, statistics, surgeries, household duties, anxiety. But in trying to make less and less, we are always somehow making more.

I struggle the most with the asymmetry of a single mastectomy. It feels more conspicuous—and neither here nor there. I keep picturing a volcano—Vesuvius threatening on the horizon.

In college I studied abroad in Florence, Italy. I lived in an apartment that was darkened every evening by the shadow of the Duomo and shook each morning with the bells of San Lorenzo. I learned to paint nudes and to appreciate pietàs and frescos. I jumped on the ferry to Elba and standing-room-only trains to Venice and Rome and beyond with just my Walkman and a small leather backpack. I hitchhiked into the Tuscan countryside and careened through the dark streets of Florence with strange boys to buy hash from the North African drug dealers who huddled in the quiet square off the Piazza della Signoria. Age nineteen: I was basically the world's most worldly person. Oh—and an expert in Chianti and Brunello.

Then, after I'd been living in Italy nearly two months, my mom came to visit.

From almost second one, we fought: my apartment was shockingly messy, my skin was greasy, what are you wearing, why are you upset, oh my God stop looking at the map in public.

We were both devastated by our rift. I'd been counting down the days to her visit for weeks. I'd missed her so badly I ached at night. The highlight of each week had been Sunday calls home — navigating my international calling card on the single payphone in the grungy lobby of my building, savoring and resenting the minutes as they ticked down toward zero.

I was stunned that she did not think I was quite the star of the Italian universe I fancied myself. Also there was this — something we came to understand together much later: her desperately needing to still be my mom, my desperately needing to prove to her how much I didn't need a mom.

We argued and sniped through the Uffizi, in front of the *David*, on the Spanish steps, under the baroque fresco in Sant'Ignazio, in a restaurant housed inside a cave in Orvieto, at a Vivaldi concert.

In my midtwenties, I tried to write a poem about the experience: the two of us bickering our way down the ancient, uneven streets of Pompeii with Vesuvius lurking behind us. It's a weird off-kilter poem, one I've never really felt like I have nailed. But years later she told me she wanted me to read it at her funeral.

See: She is dying.

It is weird to write that — like I'm saying something bad about her behind her back. But it's true. And no one knows it better than her.

Eight years of cancer. They told her she had five years when she was first diagnosed. New drugs keep coming though, and some of them have worked—for a time. A stem cell transplant. Chemo. She got to see my brother get married and watch my kids grow. Multiple hospitalizations, endless courses of steroids, blood and platelet transfusions, five bone marrow biopsies, daily debilitating nausea and diarrhea, three failed clinical trials. She's been keeping track: five days of not feeling well to every two where she's basically okay.

We read Atul Gawande's *Being Mortal* together. Its clarity on end-of-life care shakes through me like a summer storm. I give the book to everyone I know. Much of Gawande's discussion revolves around the decision to stop treatment for cancers that seem to be relentlessly unbackdownable. Many of the stories he tells there—including his own father's death from a spinal tumor—are hard to read. But what he is working toward in his difficult exploration is unquestionably beautiful: how to distill what matters most to each of us in life in order to navigate our way toward the edge of it in a meaningful and satisfying way.

Unlike the rest of the planet, my mom's mind isn't blown. "This is what I've been saying all along," she says. "You just haven't been ready to listen."

One of the things Dr. Gawande probes in his book is how to figure out what makes a person's life worth living in order to make the most sensible choices as the end of life approaches. One man in the book says he is willing to stay alive if he can eat chocolate ice cream and watch football on TV. He will even endure high levels of pain if he can do these things. Others are happy to be alive as long as they *don't* have to experience pain. Yet another just wants to do whatever possible to attend a family wedding.

My mom and I sit on her couch and talk it out. She says for her, it's about lucidity: she wants to be able to have a conversation, feel a connection. That can help us determine how long we keep pushing blood transfusions and electrolyte replacement to keep her brain as clear-thinking as possible as the myeloma takes over.

She is asked to speak at a pre-triathlon dinner in Washington, DC, for the Leukemia & Lymphoma Society and tells a ballroom of stricken-looking athletes: *Sometimes the most important thing is knowing when to quit. Sometimes being heroic is knowing when to say enough is enough.* They don't ask her to come back next year. Maybe they know she won't be here anymore.

Her latest news: The current clinical trial she's on is not working at all. The blood work is all going in the wrong direction. And this week she does say enough is enough. She doesn't want to do any more treatment.

My mom: my map, my Sistine Chapel, my *Lonely Planet*, my beautiful ruin, my volcano.

Next week—same day as my mastectomy—she is scheduled to visit Duke to see her oncologist, Dr. Gasparetto, another larger-than-life doctor: nearly six feet tall, tsunami of black hair, stiletto heels, an Italian accent that makes even the most toxic chemotherapies sound like heartbreaking arias—she pronounces the common myeloma drug thalidomide as *ta-lidio-MY-da*. The plan is to ask her how exactly one goes about dying from multiple myeloma. Whatever she says, it will sound like a song.

And I'll be five floors above, drifting through the undreaming dreamscape of anesthesia. I keep thinking about my painting teacher in Florence—a watercolor class in a timeless glass ceilinged studio on the Via dell'Alloro.

"You must promise to only follow this advice in watercolor—not in anything else in your life—well, maybe cooking," she told us. "Intensify slowly. Use lots of water, and lay down a wash of color. Walk away, let the pigment move and bleed and dry on the paper. Then return to it with a slightly deeper hue, again and again until you think you are satisfied. Whatever you do, don't rush it. The best parts happen when you have stepped away."

Surgery, anesthesia: a stepping away of sorts. A break from treatment: definitely a stepping away. But leaving treatment: This is something entirely different. She never really told us how to know when the painting was done.

Of course: *Only in watercolor* she made us promise, a roomful of American girls not yet twenty.

Thinking about it, Pompeii and cancer actually have a fair amount in common—although we fight far less on this tour. Both places are full of ghosts and surprising, palpable reminders of life interrupted midliving: loaves of bread still in the oven, unfinished art, Vesuvius not quite dormant above the city.

The last couple lines of that failed poem: You reached out to me for balance / even though we weren't speaking / and a minute later I had to do the same.

6. Pilgrim

Cool spring days, and I head out into the rain from our house down toward the greenway and the park.

Tita and I followed the exact path the other morning. The neighborhood was fierce: blossoms and sunshine and fragrant mulch and my blood coursing with steroids. Our pace was the babble of second opinions, counseling for kids, the possibilities of meditation, single or double mastectomy, disfigurement of the female form and the horror of mirrors, reconstruction: to build again or not.

I was breathless and full and grateful for clear-thinking friendship and conversation.

Today, I walk it alone. All is changed. In the grass, a brown bunny waits still as a yard ornament. And I notice the world's littlest mud puddles filling the name "Thomas" carved into the concrete path and a bed of purple lilies taller than children and the creek entirely strange from all the rain. Its strong current beneath the footbridge builds to angry rapids at the wide bend by the storm drain.

In his essay *Nature*, Emerson says, "Who looks upon a river in a meditative hour, and is not reminded of the flux of all things?" With solitude and a rainstorm: All is changed.

My parents did not bring me up in a church-going tradition. But nature is church, my great-great-great grandfather believed—

and I was raised to go into the woods. "[Nature] always speaks of Spirit. It suggests the absolute. It is a perpetual effect. It is a great shadow pointing always to the sun behind us. . . . The happiest man is he who learns from nature the lesson of worship."

He taught his children to go into the woods for communion — and they taught theirs to do the same, and so on.

"I actually hate nature," I once confided to my mom when I was about nine after a buggy week at Audubon camp. I preferred to cozy up with a book or use my stuffed animals to act out scenes from *Little Women.*

"Ha," she laughed. "Just don't ever let anyone from Dad's side of the family hear you say that. You'll probably be excommunicated."

The thing is, Emerson himself probably would have been fine with it. As his son wrote, RWE's "own attitude in the matter was, that it was only a question for each person where the best church was, — in the solitary wood, the chamber, the talk with the serious friend, or in hearing the preacher."

To be honest, growing up I didn't much care for Emerson either. In his portraits he looked bossy and a little stern. I didn't understand his essays or poems at all, although my teachers often assumed I would when they discovered my heritage. As an aspiring writer, I kept a detailed thought journal and a record of all the books I read, just as I'd been told he did — and I memorized a number of his poems. But I was a faker: I cared way more about what was happening in the Baby-Sitters Club series and what I could do to my bangs with a curling iron.

Something shifted in college at UNC. I began walking outside again—on the deep woodsy paths that surround Chapel Hill—and I took a small seminar-style class on nineteenth-century American literature. I didn't mention my Emerson connection. I discovered the beautiful, intimate, messy honesty of his journals as a way to start loving his writing.

This morning on my walk—with the creek full and all the wildlife energized by the rain—I'm thinking about an essay by another one of my favorite writers, Annie Dillard: "Seeing" from her book *Pilgrim at Tinker Creek*. There she writes: "It's all a matter of keeping my eyes open." Dillard enters nature with a giant Emersonian eye—reverent, rhapsodic—almost ecclesiastic. She reminds us again and again to clear our vision of expectations, to try to see without understanding.

Pilgrim is a beautiful word. I love the thin rhyming *i* sounds in both syllables. And the surprising seriousness of "grim." It's from the Latin *peregrinus*—meaning foreign. Same root as peregrine, like the falcon. Bird of prey, fastest member of the animal kingdom. Adventure married to strength and purpose—tinged with the strange.

Growing up in Massachusetts, *pilgrim* meant pageants with songs and construction paper buckle hats and white collars. Also: field trips to Plymouth Plantation and cramped old ships and too much salt-water taffy on the bus ride home.

Later, in college, reading *The Pilgrim's Progress*—that desperate, tortured journey, I associated it with the idea of walking with sacred purpose. The idea of seeking. The ominous landmarks: the Valley of Humiliation, the Doubting Castle. There is always room and time for a journey: Every road trip of my twenties justified in this way. Emerson called the guest room in his house the Pilgrim's Chamber. Some of its prominent pilgrim residents: Margaret Fuller, Thoreau.

"After thousands of years we're still strangers to darkness, fearful aliens in an enemy camp with our arms crossed over our chests," Dillard writes in "Seeing" as she watches dusk come to Tinker Creek, night knitting an "eyeless mask" over her face.

When it comes to illness, dying, death—those darknesses—it seems we are still so very much Plymouth Pilgrims—all fear and fretting and fortifications, and a strong sense of our own alienness in a hostile land. We don't begin to know what to do with ourselves. We cross our arms over our chests and try to look on the bright side as we starve.

I think the tumors in my breast are getting bigger instead of smaller. They ache. They protrude. At least I imagine that they do. One more month: I can hardly wait to get them out.

One of the best things I've read about that puritanical pilgrim lot is that—aside from God—they really loved wine and clean laundry.

My favorite pilgrim is the poet Anne Bradstreet. She was torn from her homeland and family and she spent three months seasick belowdecks coming to America. She suffered smallpox, paralysis, and tuberculosis. She gave birth to eight children in ten years—and they all lived. She was the first woman to publish a book of poems in the New World (at age thirty-eight), despite being relegated by her community to an intensely domestic role. And she gave her poems wonderful solid names like "By Night when Others Soundly Slept" and "Verses upon the Burning of our House, July 10th, 1666" and "A Letter to her Husband, Absent upon Publick Employment."

She and her husband arrived from England with Governor John Winthrop and his company of Puritans on June 14, 1630, on the flagship *Arbella*—a ship that reportedly carried three times as much alcohol as water on its passage across the Atlantic. Nearly all ten thousand gallons of wine had been consumed by the time they set their sea-weary feet on soil in Salem, Massachusetts.

Before they left England—as they waited anchored just off-shore aboard the ship for the right weather conditions to begin their crossing—a small group of them braved the white-capped swells to row back to Yarmouth to scrub clean their linen necker-chiefs one last time before setting out for the ultimate wilderness. I just love that. It's a beautiful, human kind of coping.

Clean laundry, wine.

Tonight John has gone to the bar to meet some friends. *Emergency beer.* He needs this as badly as I need the mastectomy. I can feel the *Arbella* tacking through the night toward my kitchen window. Stack of dishes to dry, my children to fold into their beds, but enter

Anne Bradstreet: both of us so far from home in this kitchen. Neither of us can feel ground beneath our feet. We stand at the dining room table sorting clean laundry. "These towels are so soft and warm," she marvels, sipping from her glass. Her husband is up on deck spotting some green shore, and mine is down the hill at the bar like a pin on a map of a place I've visited.

John Winthrop noted in his journal that before they ever saw the New World, they smelled it: "so pleasant a sweet ether, as did much refresh us, & there came the smell off the shore like the smell of a garden."

Pilgrim. *Peregrinus.* Foreigner. I am trying to uncross my arms in the darkness. I am trying to keep my eyes open.

Early this afternoon on the back deck there was a ruckus in the upper branches of the giant oak. Two or three crows were loudly mobbing a hawk, and the hawk was sitting on the branch stoically ignoring the whole to-do. *What is this?* I was thinking. *Couldn't that hawk make mincemeat of those crows in about three seconds if it chose to?* But then in a minute or so it was over—the crows having moved on, the hawk still perched on the branch, its genius eyes working the horizon.

I'm terrified. I'm fine. The world is changed and exactly as before. There are crows in my hair. I have no hair. Bring me a jug of wine. Bring me a kerchief to scrub spotlessly clean.

7. Damaged Goods

My friend Ginny who lives down in Charleston has the same kind of breast cancer as I do, and we like to text each other with ideas for a line of morbid prefab cancer patient thank-you cards to real and imaginary people that Ginny calls the "casscrolc bitches." She's a trust and estates lawyer, so she's an expert in casserole bitches and their eyelash batting.

Our business is going to be called Damaged Goods and we plan to leave our children wealthy.

Thank you for the taco casserole. It worked even better than my stool softeners.

Thoughts and prayers are great, but Ativan and pot are better.

Thank you for the flowers. I hope they die before I do.

All your phone messages about how not knowing exactly what's going on with me has stressed you out really helped me put things in perspective.

Xanax is white, Zofran is blue, steroids make me feel like throttling you.

When they found Ginny's cancer, a few weeks after they found mine, it had already jumped into one of her lymph nodes. Ginny is a Carolina grad just like I am, so naturally she named her evil cancerous node after Tar Heel nemesis Christian Laettner. Neither of us know what to make of relying on Duke to save my life. She named her breast tumor after another famous Dookie, Bobby Hurley. "The chemo is going to blast those motherfuckers to obscurity," she texts.

8. Drama

Nine p.m., and my half-front-toothed older son is loitering in our bedroom after his nightly insulin shot. He's pretending to tell me about an idea he had for a comic book, but he keeps stealing looks at the TV screen, paused in Netflix binge mode on the Watch the Next Episode screen with the little text teaser below.

CHASING LIFE: Episode 12. April's cancer goes into remission, but her return to work isn't as smooth. Meanwhile, Leo languishes in a coma.

"So, you're watching a cancer show?" he finally says sheepishly. "Why would you do that?"

"I don't know," I say. "I guess it makes me feel a little more normal. Plus it has really terrible writing, so it makes me laugh."

"Terrible how?" he asks.

"Terrible like characters bawling, 'Well, maybe you forgot, but I have *cancer!!!*'"

"Oh," he says. "That kind of terrible. Like, 'Calm down. We know. We're sorry about your cancer but please stop yelling.'"

"Yes," I say. "Just like that."

9. Geography

On the latest mammogram images, it looks like you're staring down from an airplane at night. The two tumors are lit-up cities— say Greensboro and Winston-Salem. And the four-centimeter stretch between them is Interstate 40, illuminated by headlights. We won't know exactly how trafficky I-40 is until the surgeon gets in there.

According to Dr. Cavanaugh, this is a stupid way for cancer to behave. Smart cancer explodes itself like an atom bomb— mushrooming out wherever possible and jumping on the lymph node train to ride to the far reaches of the body and set up diabolic satellite campuses there. Stupid cancer makes a tumor, gets bored, sidles around, builds a nearby tumor. We hope.

Cavanaugh is not afraid of saying things like *hopefully cured* and *probably no more chemo*. But she also sends me for more imaging—the packed room of anxious women ranging from twenty to ninety all in our identical gray dressing gowns, half of us texting, half knitting—*just to confirm the geography*, as she says. As though having a map makes the trail less snowy.

10. The Wolf's Lair

Here's how the doctors will figure out whether or not your cancer has likely spread: The day before surgery, under an imaging machine in a cold basement room, a needle will be inserted into your tumor and you will be injected with a blue radioactive isotope dye.

As the stinging wears off, you will lie very still. The machine will be the only one that speaks to you — a robot voice commanding you to breathe.

Next, you will be sent off to have some lunch. You will sit in the sun on the patio of the Cancer Café eating a turkey wrap and watching a couple your parents' age, both in wheelchairs, one of whom has become tangled in his oxygen lines, the other of whom is tenderly unwrapping the line from where it is caught in the wheel as she holds her cigarette aloft.

Later, back in the basement, a radiologist will track the path of the isotope with a Geiger counter. Whatever surrounding lymph nodes light up will be the nodes the tumor most likely drains to — the sentinel nodes — therefore, the ones most likely to contain escaping cancer cells. They will still be lit up when the surgeon goes in there the next day.

These are the ones he will pop out and send off to the pathologist who will chop and smear and stain them onto slides to examine under the microscope in a darkened room like your two sons memorizing dinosaur books and baseball cards with flashlights after lights out.

Only one node lights up during the sentinel-node mapping. Lone sentinel at the castle gate.

"Is that bad?" I ask the tech.

"There is no good or bad," he says. He sounds tired. "It just means you have one sentinel."

"I have no guard or sentinel but the stars," said Montaigne, noting how the heavily guarded homes of his neighbors were frequently attacked — and his was not. "My home is closed to none who knock upon its gate, with only a doorman as guardian — and 'guardian' only in the old-fashioned sense; he serves less to defend my fate than to present it with greater elegance and grace."

Montaigne would have sent my sentinel home as well, I guess — off into the misty, Aquitaine night. No locks, for him. No guards, no food tasters.

I'm rereading the Montaigne biography. Age thirty-eight was a big year for him as well: Following his father's death a couple years earlier, he retired from public life in Bordeaux, where he had been a well-known statesman, sequestered himself on his family estate in the countryside, and started work on his famous essays.

"Don't you think it's wild that Montaigne never had a food

tester—given how politically prominent he was during such a fractious time?" I ask John.

"It's very him. Montaigne the Stoic," he says. "I bet your Puritan ancestors wouldn't have had food tasters either. Nothing cures a dose of poison like a stiff upper lip and a brisk walk."

John loves Montaigne as much as I do. He's the first person who told me to read him. "But really, I think it's only serious despots that have food tasters. The Emperor Claudius, Hitler, Vladimir Putin. Probably Donald Trump. The guilty ones."

I slip down an Internet rabbit hole one morning reading about the life of Margot Woelk, the only one of Hitler's fifteen food tasters—his conscripted "poison brigade"—to survive the war. She's almost a hundred now:

"The food was delicious . . . asparagus, bell peppers, everything you can imagine," she tells the interviewer about their menu in the bunker. The wild, fresh flavors of peacetime. "But . . . we could never enjoy [it]."

An armed bus would pick her up each morning from her mother-in-law's house, and she was taken to a barracks in a nearby town where the food was prepared to be taken to Hilter's *Wolfsschanze* headquarters—the Wolf's Lair. The tasting took place each day between 11:00 a.m. and noon.

She remembers crying in terror with each bite, seated with the other single Aryan girls around a wooden table guarded by the SS. For two and a half years. Sometimes girls would drop to the floor in agony, but it was from anxiety not poison.

Seven decades later, Margot has apparently kept the habit of eating in tiny, cautious bites. In one article I find, she is nibbling the crumbs of a coffee cake as she talks to the journalist.

Although she never saw Hitler in person, she says she despised the person she risked her life for every day. *He was a really repugnant man. And a pig.*

I was led here by the metaphor—*let the castle be unlocked*—but now I can't hold it straight. Am I Hitler? Or is Hitler the tumor? This isn't even a metaphor, is it? It's only a different hard story. But Margot and I have one thing in common: our bodies. Our bodies are not our own. Hers was requisitioned by the SS; mine by illness, medicine.

"Where will your breast go," Freddy asks, "you know, after they cut it off."

"Probably a drawer in a basement lab somewhere at Duke," I say. "Well, they keep the tumor for future testing, but I guess they maybe throw out the breast."

John teases me later. "That's a great image for a kid to have in his head. Emotional Trauma for five hundred please, Alex."

"What in the world was I supposed to say?" I ask. I never know what I am supposed to say. Honestly: neither does John. We look into getting therapists for the kids. "It would be so awesome if *someone* knew the right things to say," I text Ginny. Ginny's kids are two years older than mine. Her daughter, eleven, on the cusp of understanding everything. "Amen," she says.

After the surgery, when John and I walk together down a corridor at Duke, he'll sometimes make his voice all high-pitched and eerie. "Niii-na, where are you? It's your breast here. I miss you. Hellllp meee, Niii-na."

Try to see without understanding. The first time I see a surgical drain up close is about a week before the mastectomy in the breast clinic waiting room. I have no idea what it is. *It's all a matter of keeping my eyes open.* A very young woman, maybe twenty-five, chatting with the receptionist, with two clear bulbs clipped to a glittery belt on her jeans, a liquid-filled tube looping down at her hips on each side and then disappearing up under her shirt. They are filled with a brilliant orange-red fluid that looks like Gatorade. She starts to laugh really hard, then catches herself, touching the juice-filled bulbs tenderly. "Aw, man," jokes the receptionist. "Sucks when you can't even laugh." *Our arms crossed over our chests.*

11. Memory of Elephants

Like a school of fish or a pride of lions or a murder of crows, a group of elephants is called a "memory." A memory of elephants.

Nothing thunderous in that phrase—nothing like what is suggested by a herd of elephants or a parade of elephants. More like elephants drinking from a low lake at sunrise. Or a spot where elephants used to be drinking, but are no longer. Something enormous and consuming and ethereal.

Not unlike anesthesia, really, which—as the absence of all sensation—leaves you with incisions and deep aches and crisp bandages you cannot empirically account for and are therefore compelled to make sense of by conjuring a collection of massive and unshakable dreamlike certainties.

Surgery goes smoothly. Beforehand, my parents slip upstairs before my mom's appointment with Dr. Gasparetto to send me off into the spinning nothingness.

John is right next to me when I wake up—and then fall back asleep—and wake up again—and conk out again. His mom has flown in from Oregon to watch our kids back in Greensboro. "They're doing great," he says. "They're having a blast. They haven't asked about you once."

He massages my hand, smiles at my dopiness, and makes fun of me on social media: *Nina is doing great and she's higher than a Gary Busey convention. Her first description of her "new body" was*

to look down her hospital gown, look up, hold up one finger and say
"uno; not dos."

The sound of the Pirates playing an evening game on a distant TV in a distant universe seems to sift like light through the hospital blinds as I slowly reenter the world.

And then there is my surgeon peering down at me, telling me what an excellent job he has done and that my sentinel node looks negative and making jokes I can't follow even though I'm pretty sure they are the same jokes he was making before surgery.

On the subject of elephants, the recovery room feels full of them — a memory of elephants.

There is the cancer elephant: What will the lymph node tell us when it returns from pathology? Another elephant: Where *is* my missing breast? We have *uno* not *dos*. And then my mom's elephant, that unpredictable beast, which shrinks and grows, sometimes looking familiar, but other times so strange and coarse I think it is actually a rhinoceros — part of a crash of rhinos, or a stubbornness of rhinos.

"Phew," my mom says when she hears the good lymph node news. "I couldn't bear checking out of this life without knowing you were going to be okay."

A gaze of raccoons. A rhumba of rattlesnakes. A float of crocodiles. A rafter of turkeys. A business of ferrets. An exaltation of skylarks. Groups of animals fill the room, and I drift back to sleep.

I haven't seen under the bandage yet — that foreign land, that new world. It does not seem obviously gory or bruised or swollen. (The surgeon did, in fact, do a great job.) But I don't know what it is. It looks flat, almost concave—like a lake bed where a memory of elephants once drank. It is an absence, a memory itself.

Right now my emotions around it are waiting as if on a shelf just out of reach. Right now the focus is completely physical, almost geographical. Right now: the drain in my chest, the sore armpit, the way my shirts sag on one side.

But there are all the other things, too—the obliterated sense of femininity, the skewing of self, the strangeness of the body. I can't quite find the terms to understand that part yet. I guess that's why this fact is so very elephantine right now. It's definitely there, but I can't seem to figure out what to say about it yet.

So right now I train my eye on these dreamlike certainties: A cure of doctors will examine me in the morning. And in the meantime, a cauldron of thunderstorms simmers on the horizon and an anticipation of cocktails awaits some ice.

12. Reconnoitering the Edge

Before he was conscripted into the family investment firm, my great-grandfather Raymond Emerson worked as a civil engineer and surveyor in the American West.

I never met him—he died the year I was born—but my dad remembers him as a strange, brilliant, unsettling—and later demented—man who lost his mind maybe because he was forced to return to the button-down East Coast establishment. Or maybe because he spent a lifetime chewing on an old lead bullet.

My most concrete and only intimate experience of him is the house he designed and built in the 1930s on the side of a remote bluff on an island off the Massachusetts coast where I have spent every summer of my life. It's a simple house—long and sturdy and rustic with a memorable roofline and ample porches—in a dramatic, isolated spot, with a view almost as expansive as a Western skyline. It looks like it would be more at home perched on a prairie or at the edge of a canyon than staring out at sailboats and Martha's Vineyard.

When I'm there, I imagine him pacing out the house site on the empty hill—thinking it through in the tall grasses, his feet learning the contours and challenges of the land. The house is clearly one designed by a man who loved the outdoors above all else, and cared less for interiors. It is a portrait of his formidable grandfather Ralph Waldo Emerson that dominates the mantel inside.

Just yards from the house there is a drop-off into the Sound that everyone in my family has come to know as a kind of defining edge—where we've measured our steps in the dark. Where I've measured the thought that in the dark there is no bluff, only me and the noise of the bluff, the luff of the end, the bellow of something else beginning.

Although it is the family of my great-grandmother Amelia Forbes—Raymond Emerson's wife—through whom the island has been passed down, Ralph Waldo Emerson came to the island at least a few times in his life as a family friend and in-law. I am not sure that he preferred this stark, exposed seashore to his quiet Concord woods, but he wrote his poem "Waldeinsamkeit" here. *Waldeinsamkeit* is the untranslatable German word for the feeling of divine solitude and contemplation in the woods. Church in the woods.

Like my great-grandfather Emerson, my mom only started coming here when she married into the family. But nevertheless she has always said she would like to have some of her ashes spread up on this hill. Lately I am imagining this act in more detail.

The other night, in a fit of irritation and optimism, I tore out one of my surgical drains, and this evening the last of the Steri-Strips un-gooed itself. Now, for the first time since the mastectomy I am free of all the accompanying apparatus—all the not-me stuff—and I feel like I can finally get a decent sense of the landscape. I am pacing it out. I am reconnoitering the edge.

Here are my untrained surveyor's notes:

I hadn't really noticed before, but the scar is a stretched S-shape — kind of a meandering river — snaking about eight inches from my sternum to just under my armpit. John sees a sideways Superman-type S. I see a lazy question mark with no dot. The whole area is numb, so tracing it with my fingers is the disorienting gap between the expected and the perceived. It is not lovely, exactly, but it is — to my fingers — the new world. I cannot stop wanting to know it better.

Ralph Waldo Emerson of course read Montaigne, too — and revered him as an example of healthy skepticism. Skeptic — from the classical Greek *skeptesthai*: to search, implying searching but not finding. Not a skeptic as in a nonbeliever, but rather, in RWE's words, "the considerer, the prudent, taking in sail, counting stock, husbanding his means, believing that a man has too many enemies than that he can afford to be his own foe."

"I would rather have a good understanding of myself than of Cicero," says Montaigne. He writes in great detail of his diet, his bowel habits, exercise, sex, his aches and pains, his kidney stones. "I study myself more than any other subject. That is my metaphysics; that is my physics."

"You may read theology, and grammar, and metaphysics elsewhere," Emerson writes about Montaigne's work. "Whatever you get here shall smack of the earth and of real life, sweet, or smart, or stinging."

Relentless searching, while at the same time unattached to the outcome of whatever is discovered. John is reading in bed. I shut the door to the bathroom, remove my towel, stand at the vanity.

The terrain around the scar seems to be treacherous in some stretches, flat in others, with a fine ridge that slopes through the shallow crater of my right chest. The skin puckers near the incision in folds that remind me of my nipple after nursing: the baby's head lolling back, the skin of the breast newly pliable and soft. There is no scar tissue there—just a thin strand that disappears into the freckles of my chest like a line of thought that bears forgetting.

"Cut these words, and they would bleed; they are vascular and alive," says Emerson of the Frenchman's writing style. Montaigne the surgeon: He probes and dissects and biopsies the thought. Chops and stains the slide, retrieves the microscope from the shelf. Montaigne the pathologist. "The sincerity and marrow of the man reaches to his sentences," says Emerson.

My remaining breast looks as ridiculous there as I imagined it would. Vesuvius rumbling over burned Pompeii. "Death everywhere mingles with and is blended into our lives," Montaigne writes in his forties. "Decline foreshadows its hour and intrudes into our onward course itself. I have portraits of my appearance at twenty-five and thirty-five; if I compare them with the present what a difference! How much farther is my present image from these than from my dying!"

I have recently turned thirty-eight. The hair that pokes through my scalp is white. I am pale from the opiates, from recovering indoors. I cannot yet lift my arm. I am a ghost of myself at thirty-five, at twenty-five. *How much farther?* Montaigne's famous motto: *Que sais-je?* What do I know? I trace the scar again with my finger. *Unattached to outcome,* I try saying out loud in front of the mirror.

We have called in hospice for my mom.

It's strange, because *hospice* is one of those words that when you say it people's faces fall. It is a word that evokes last breaths and hushed voices. But the more I think about it, the more I'm struck by what a beautiful word it is—*hospice.* It *is* hushed, especially at the end. But it's comfortable and competent sounding, too. A French word with Latin roots—very close to hospital but with so much more serenity due to those S sounds. (You see, I am growing increasingly fond of the letter S.)

It used to mean a rest house for travelers—for pilgrims. And is there anything more welcome to a weary pilgrim than rest?

Some more surveyor's notes:

I get the full pathology back from the mastectomy. They have found the two tumors they expected in there—along with eight centimeters of noninvasive cancer in the ducts. The sentinel nodes are negative and the margins are clear although only clear by a tenth of a millimeter. The tumors have not shrunk in any measurable way, so unfortunately the verdict on the chemo is that it just wasn't that effective.

Dr. Cavanaugh wants to do further pathology and consult with her colleagues for input on my case. From there I suppose we'll get a sense of the new landscape and what to expect as we pace about in the tall grass.

Tracing my fingers again and again over the scar, I've realized that something is familiar. It isn't a Superman S—or a question mark, or even a river. It's a path—a path I know pretty well. It's the one that starts in the weedy cove down by the boathouse, weaves its way past the cat briar and beach roses, and starts to climb up the hill through grass thick with berries and ticks and poison ivy, curving gently this way and that up the bluff to the house where I can see just now my mother is gliding out of sight, stepping from the southwest porch in through the sliding door.

13. Party Sampler

On nights when John and I can get a sitter we often gather in Tita and Drew's writing shed in their backyard with a playmate of ice and some handles of liquor and a party sampler of Pepperidge Farm cookies and John deejays us through eighties and nineties dance grooves on his cell phone and we pretend we are childless. Tita and Drew have their kids asleep in the house on the baby monitor.

Both of them are writing professors, and this semester Drew is teaching a class of freshmen who he swears hate him.

"I lose them a little more every time I open my mouth," he tells us. "I told them that before they could be writers they had to go out and get their hearts broken a little bit. They looked back at me with what I can only call disgust and pity."

"We are disgusting and pitiful," I say. "And broken. We are so broken we count as the adults now."

John, who hates to dance, pulls me to my feet when "Take My Breath Away," starts playing and sways me in his arms. Tita and Drew do the same. We are laughing. We are tired. We are drunk.

"Take me to bed or lose me forever," says John. My back aches, my chest hurts, and the old chemo nausea is rising in my chest. "Show me the way home," I say.

14. The Toll Collector

Benny turns six. Last year's passions: cats, baseball, Lionel Messi, outboard engines. This year: tollbooths, windmills, livestock, and black holes. He's a tough kid to shop for. The recommended picks on our Amazon account look like we are planning to survive some sort of road-trip apocalypse.

During one of the several candle-extinguishing ceremonies, Benny whispers to me that his birthday wish is that he could be a tollbooth operator when he gets older and that my breast would grow back someday without any cancer in it.

I hope for both of these things as well (kid with a job, no more cancer)—and neither of them (a less exhaust-filled job, no mutant body parts). But I'm glad these are his wishes. They are a very Benny version of what I would have wished for if they were my candles—the same wish I make every year: that everyone I love will find what makes them happy and that the universe will keep them safe.

John arranges a birthday surprise visit to the tollbooth in the parking garage where he works. Carl, the parking attendant, hoists Benny up into the seat and shows him the register.

"This is where you put all the money people give you, huh?" says Benny—giant grin, swiveling in the seat. Carl has a clip-on fan in the booth and a couple of books—the Bible, a Danielle

Steel paperback. Carl has told John that the Bible belonged to his father, who fought with General Patton in World War II. "Every battle Patton was in my dad was there, too, with the Bible in his pocket keeping him safe."

"You know I don't get to keep any of that money, right, little man?" Carl says to Benny.

"Yes," says Benny solemnly. "I've heard that."

Carl shows him how to operate the lever that lifts the arm of the tollbooth. "That's how the magic works."

"I just cannot believe I am only six and I have already sat in a real, live tollbooth," says Benny as we drive away.

Days later John tells me that every time Carl sees him now he laughs and shakes his head. "Didn't know I was such a celebrity!"

One day he says, "Your wife sure likes to keep her hair real short."

"Yeah," says John. "Chemo."

Carl says, "I was worried you were gonna say that, so I've been praying for her every day just in case." From then on, he tells John I'm in his prayers every time he pushes the magic lever to raise the arm, every time John passes through.

15. Nowhere

John hates change, and cancer is change run amok. "Can't we please just opt out of this whole cancer thing?" he asks one night in bed.

"Nope," I say. "And you have to love me even more now. You're not allowed to leave your bald, one-breasted wife. That's very gauche."

"Just tell me where I'm allowed to put my hands so I don't hurt you," he says during sex.

"Nowhere," I say.

16. Personals

One day Ginny texts: "Here's a new card for our collection: *Thanks so much for coming to visit and fucking my husband. I needed a divorce to keep my mind off cancer.*"

The visitor in question is one of her close friends from college who has come to help take care of her during chemo. A new level of casserole bitch. She catches them in the living room one night when she gets up to get a glass of water. Ginny goes into lawyer-warrior mode. She makes them sign affidavits before they even get up from the fold-out sofa.

I have no idea what to say. I spend days scowling at every man I see. For the first time in all of this, I can't sleep. John sees the silver lining: "I'm really looking better and better, aren't I?"

I text Ginny: "You are fully entitled to slap the next person who tells you that God only gives us what we can handle."

The day after the divorce finalizes she writes: "I've decided I'm going to take out a personal ad on craigslist." We've been bemoaning our post-treatment bodies. "One-boobed, mentally unstable, newly divorced, borderline obese freight train with cankles, two kids, a silver-fox butch hairdo, and vaginal dryness ISO hot-bodied twentysomething with a large trust fund and larger hands who likes long walks on the beach, intelligent discussion, and uncomfortable sex."

I think of a match immediately: Montaigne. His middle-aged

111

craigslist ad (not that he was on the market—his wife glimmers into view from time to time): Straight-ish White Aristocrat/Thinker with persistent kidney stones and gout, robust bowels and waning sexual appetite, impressive book collection in welcoming medieval tower, and a passion for the Ancients and spicy food, ISO moderation in everything, long walks in unsettled woods, and intimacy with fear. Bandits, skeletons, and Death welcome. Politicians and doctors need not respond.

The man dreaded medical inventions as much as Ginny and I do: "To be subject to both kidney stones and abstention from the pleasure of eating oysters: that is two evils in one," he wrote. "The illness pinches us on one side; the remedy on the other."

The illness, the remedy. We are such fragile creatures, although we feel far more like oysters until we are dying—those rough husks.

Like Montaigne, Ginny has always lived not far from the coast—for her: the low country down in South Carolina. On one visit, she takes me out shell collecting with our kids and I can hardly believe the bounty: The *lettered olive*, she teaches me, looks like a rolled bill—smooth and heavy in your palm, rarely found intact. There is *angel wing, moon snail, sand dollar*, and *slipper*. The *fighting conch* is a beauty—midsized and spiky, and the unrolled lip at the edge is as inviting a castle as I've ever seen.

17. Tumor Board

Tonight my dad has invited us over to eat his famous barbecued chicken, and my mom feels strong enough to come to the dinner table. Usually she eats in the room she calls "the salon," a room she had my dad paint a warm yellowy orange a few years back—where she can recline on her favorite couch next to the gas stove. She looks like a child in the dining room chair—a tiny version of herself, half-there at the head of the table, her legs curled up under her body, picking at her food, smiling at me briefly when I catch her eye.

Just as we start to eat, my phone rings. An unfamiliar Raleigh number—but I know right away who is on the other end.

"Hi, Dr. Cavanaugh!" I answer, getting up from the table.

Several days ago we went to Duke expecting answers and a plan following the mastectomy. Unfortunately there had been a delay with the pathology and the tumor board so we came home with neither.

Tumor board: the term kills me every time I hear it. *You're just saying that to freak me out*, I think. What is actually a group of doctors from different specialties discussing the specifics of your case together around a table sounds like a cancer court-martial or a torture tactic. You could call it a "patient review meeting." You could call it "checking in with my colleagues." You could call it an "exaltation of oncologists."

"I promise I'll call you right after the tumor board meets on Monday afternoon," she'd said, "But you don't have to answer the phone if you don't want to. You can always just let it go to voicemail and I'll let you know what we've decided."

She is on her way home from work, she tells me when I answer. But she wanted to call because she'd promised.

I can picture her tucked in some cool, pristine luxury sedan gliding along I-40. Unmelted iced coffee in the cup holder. Her blond hair still pulled back tidily from her face. A guided meditation CD whirring quietly in the player on pause.

The restained pathology report is back and the tumors are as we thought—only maybe not quite as dumb as we hoped. The tumor board unanimously recommends that we do another four cycles of chemo—this time with Adriamycin, a harsher drug.

And because it turns out a tenth of a millimeter margin isn't enough to let anyone breathe easy, I will also have six weeks of radiation when the chemo is done.

My hair has just started growing back and it's soft and downy and makes me feel human. My eyebrows are coming back, too— although in an incredibly disorganized way that I can kind of relate to. And I just rejoined the gym. As Dr. Cavanaugh is talking I feel like I'm hurtling backward, that I'm that many steps farther away from getting back to normal—whatever that is.

"Nina," she says as we start to hang up, "I just want you to know that I still feel like we're in a good place on this."

I'm rethinking my image of serene, smooth-sailing Dr. Cavanaugh. It is 7 p.m. on a Monday night. She is headed home after a long day discussing tumors and telling patients who wouldn't just let their phones go to voicemail that they need more chemo. Maybe worse. At home: her kids—two, not much older than mine, hastily crafted dinner, a mountain of email, a bag unpacked from the conference she returned from late last night. She probably used the only quiet moments of her whole day to call me from the highway.

One time she told me about lying in her son's bed while he asked her questions about how to ask a girl to a dance. I like to picture her in the dark like that, her head on his pillow, her confident, firm voice steadying the night. I can imagine exactly what it would feel like. It is a remarkable thing to feel the hug of the world keeping you safe—almost like standing out in the middle of six lanes of a chaotic highway, but tucked inside the pod of a tollbooth.

When I come back to the dinner table, my mom has disappeared—the food on her plate barely touched. John and my dad are doling out dessert to the kids. I find her lying on the couch in the salon. "I'm okay," she says, not opening her eyes. "Now tell me all about Dr. Cavanaugh's latest plan to save the day."

18. Hospice

I answer the door the first time the hospice nurse comes to visit my parents' house. My mom is perched in the salon and my dad is making lunch. The kids are playing Wild West out in the yard—riding two tipped-over garbage cans as horses and wielding lassos. "Eat my dust, partner," Freddy is yelling. Benny is squealing and neighing.

"Oh my!" the hospice nurse says, with a smile that suggests she is more used to the hushed version of her job. "Ms. Riggs! It's wonderful to meet you. I didn't realize you had young kids."

She thinks I'm my mom. She's noted the baldness and the surgical drain hanging clipped to my shirt that had to be reinstalled when my mastectomy site kept filling and refilling with fluid.

"Oh no, I'm the daughter," I say. "Sorry. I know it's confusing." Her smile wavers and also softens a little. "I'll show you to my mom."

Imagine this: Even hospice nurses retain a sense of the way the world should work.

19. The Blade

Book club moves from the living room to the salon so my mom can lie down on her couch while we discuss. We have just read a graphic novel we all loved—chosen in part because she is struggling to focus when there is too much text—but I can't relax. All I can think about is the part at the end of the discussion when we pick a date for our next meeting.

I know that everyone in book club knows that the hospice nurse has suggested that given her status, my mom probably has about a month to six weeks left—but I'm wondering if they remember. I am panicking at the thought of choosing a date that she isn't around for any longer. I feel like I'm six years old and about to be caught in some horrible lie—hurtling like an egg through midair. And I'm shocked at my inability to say something out loud to confront it, diffuse it even: *So do they have book club in the afterlife?*

I am positive that the possibility that she won't live to see our next meeting is not lost on her either, but she seems distracted tonight—disconnected from the discussion.

"Are you okay?" I mouth to her.

She nods, but then winces. "Can you ask Dad to bring me in my pain pills?"

Then quickly to everyone else: "Don't go, don't go! This is just a new version of me having another glass of wine." She never wants the party to end.

Anne saves the day: "Seems like many of us will be unavailable for the month of August with summer vacations and all. Wouldn't it be easier to leave the date open-ended for now?"

Linda saves it again: "And maybe it would be fun for each of us to just come and report on our favorite book from the last year, from book club or not."

Tita nudges my arm as we stand to leave. "Call me when you get home if you want to talk."

Of course they all remember; of course it is not only me, trying to both preserve and crack open the lie that time doesn't pass, that loss isn't a blade so sharp that it can make you bleed long before you ever feel the sting.

My mom stays curled up on the couch, her tiny body somehow seeming to have become a little smaller over the course of the evening.

"You all be good," she is saying, starting to doze. "I love you."

These are the things we all say at the end of book club now: *I love you.* Of course we do. Why haven't we been saying that all along?

20. The Purple House

Next door to our little green bungalow is a house that has been painted deep purple for as long as I can remember, with symmetrical hot-pink pillars supporting the portico. For years, a black POW flag hung like a banner between the second-story windows.

Years back, when John and I first moved to Greensboro for me to start grad school—before we lived here in Westerwood, our current neighborhood—I remember there was also a row of impeccable toilets that lined the front yard.

At that point, I only vaguely knew that the purple spectacle was an act of protest. It had something to do with the eclectic, bungalow-y, artists-filled neighborhood being turned into a historic district with covenants and codes that would mean you needed to ask permission to paint your house a new color, among other things.

Dan, our now-neighbor—decorated Vietnam vet and one of the few black residents of our largely white neighborhood—wasn't having it. He saw the move to make a historic district as invasive of property owners' rights and thought it smacked of underhanded segregationist techniques to keep the neighborhood white and upper-middle class.

So, he and a smattering of other neighbors decided to paint their houses outlandish shades of purple. Dan's was by far the most conspicuous, though—plus the toilets. And the signs that read, Jim Crow Is Alive in Westerwood. The contrast with the architectural stateliness of his Dutch colonial house and his immaculately man-icured yard along the neighborhood's main thoroughfare gave the gesture maximum impact.

As it turns out, Westerwood never did become a historic dis-trict. But Dan also never repainted his house.

Twelve years later, the toilets and protest signs are long gone and the purple is faded, but if I'm giving directions to anyone who has lived in our town for more than a few years, all I have to say is, "We're next door to the purple house," and they know exactly where I mean.

I adore the purple house even though—and possibly because— it's not in my own nature to be conspicuous. As a bald woman, I noted stricken looks from other moms at PTA meetings and gro-cery parking lots. I noted our mailman hurrying to avoid me on the stoop. Discomfort from waiters and shop attendants. The worried brow of the guy who hands me my locker key at the gym.

I hated it. But, as my head began to resprout, I also note that baldness served a role—like mourning clothes. *I am going through something,* it announces. *Be gentle with me.*

"I miss my bald head," emails my high-school friend Christy who also did chemo this year. She's a couple months ahead of me in her treatment.

"That is one very complicated emotion," I reply.

Departing from baldness also denotes a departure from treatment. Whether cured or beyond a cure, there is still fear. Because treatment itself—effective or not—is a kind of solution. Dr. Cavanaugh says that her patients have told her that the hardest part of their treatment was the day they finished, the day they make the *see-you-in-six-months* appointment.

"I do not at all like to cure one evil by another," says Montaigne, no stranger to doctors or illness, who in one sense captures in a dozen words all of what feels wrong about cancer treatment today. "I hate remedies that are more of a nuisance than the sickness."

He would not have enjoyed chemo. But part of me argues with him here—although maybe I am the dupe. It is an unintentional side effect, but there is a dark harmony in going through treatment that I do not want to ignore either. In treatment, the wrongness I feel in my life is a wrongness reflected in my body—my steroid puffy face, my bald head, my lopsided chest. And spending my days at the cancer center: It's something I'm part of. I make sense there somehow. A lot more sense than I make at the gym or the elementary school or the grocery store or work meetings—or all the other places I've sat outside of for too long in my car taking deep breaths as I attempt to return to civilian life.

The sound I most associate with being Dan's neighbor is the leaf blower. He is at it nearly every day. He never stops moving—leaf blowing, mowing, weeding, hosing down, hammering, scrubbing, holding the line. Next to his pristine house, our low-slung not-purple craftsman looks like it was devoured by a forest.

When I was spending a lot of time bald on our back deck—in the throes of chemo and buzzed out of my mind by the steroids—thinking, gardening, breathing, trying to get my footing in a world where I suddenly didn't feel at home—I would often spend the day next to the sounds of Dan's labor on the other side of the fence.

"We have to learn that what cannot be cured must be endured," Montaigne also says. You see why I talk to him all day.

Over a period of several weeks in early summer, the deck was perpetually covered in drifts of these airy little clusters called "catkins," fallen from the willow oak in the yard. You would sweep it clean and go inside for a glass of water, and come out to find it looked like an abandoned property. You'd pick up the broom again.

One morning—in socks and pajamas and no hair—steroids, nausea, nothing tasting right, nothing looking right, nothing right to say to anyone—I stood on the deck and held the line: I kept sweeping. I could not stop any more than the catkins could stop falling from the oak. I passed the whole morning in this way, the soft skin between my thumb and pointer finger eventually worn raw.

I think of Emerson, begrudgingly snared and re-snared by his garden. In his journal he writes: "With brow bent, with firm intent, I go musing in the garden walk. I stoop to pull up a weed that is choking the corn, and find there are two; close behind it is a third, and I reach out my arm to a fourth; behind that there are four thousand and one. I am heated and untuned, and by and by wake up from my idiot dream of chickweed and red-root, to find that I with adamantine purposes am chickweed and pipergrass myself."

All that time of my sweeping, I could hear Dan puttering. For hours, he'd been slightly hunched over his patio, spraying steady lines of Roundup between the infinite bricks, eradicating the chances of anything unwanted taking root.

At one point as he walked up the back steps to his house, he paused and looked over at me sweeping—he who does not make easy eye contact even when someone is not bald in their pajamas—and we nodded at each other, as though acknowledging that the thing rattling loose in both of us was the same.

21. The Nipple Highway

I text Ginny: "I think we should consider expanding our business model to include a line of customizable photo cards so you can send your loved ones pictures of your nipple tattoos."

We've both been reading about this guy, Vinnie Myers, who is based in Maryland and New Orleans. He's apparently the grandmaster of nipple tattooing. He used to be a regular tattoo artist, but now his website says: *Many things have changed over the past few years and now I spend most of my time tattooing nipple areola tattoos on breast cancer warriors.*

His work is extraordinary, and women flock to him like pilgrims: nothing frou-frou. No flowers or dragons covering the scar. Just nipples of all varieties: pink and pubescent, dark and post-breastfeeding, large, small, one that even contains an artificial piercing. They look 3-dimensional and completely real.

We've watched videos of Vinny working. He wears hipster glasses, a tie, and a straw porkpie hat. "He is clearly our guy," I write.

"Road trip down the nipple highway," texts Ginny. "That's our reward."

Right now I don't even have a breast. The whole idea feels like an abstraction. "A kind of updated *Thelma and Louise*," I text back. "We're gonna need to get a convertible."

22. Myopia

Dying provokes nearsightedness in the caregiver.

We drive my mom back and forth to Duke, we spend long hours awaiting lab work and blood transfusions, we cancel teacher conferences and hair appointments, we administer water and pills, we greet hospice nurses, we sit at the bedside, we confer in the hallway outside her room, we wait. We become myopic about the whole thing, losing the ability to take stock of what all these efforts are about—and what they portend.

Myopia. Myopia. I keep thinking about that word. There was a polo and hunt club named Myopia near where we lived in Massachusetts, founded in 1882 by four men who were all plagued by nearsightedness—although I didn't know until much later that the name was a flourish of New England wit. The place had nothing to do with my life—we didn't ride much, even though my dad's family is "horsey"—and we definitely didn't hunt, but *myopia* always sounded pastoral and mysterious and lovely to me. I remember driving by the discreet sign and long mysterious drive along Route 1A with some regularity, and my decidedly unhorsey mother often unable to stop herself from tittering over the name.

"A la-di-da club called Myopia!" she would snark. "It doesn't get any better than that!"

My mom worked for years as a medical transcriptionist and

she always knew all the good medical terms: *fistula, ketoacidosis, decompensating, myocardial infarction.* I vaguely understood the eccentric discontinuity of a fox hunting club named after the condition of being nearsighted, but I didn't really get the bigger social-class implications of not seeing the forest for the trees until decades later. She would have appreciated knowing that one of the club's founding members was my dad's maternal great-great grandfather, John Murray Forbes—something I discover when I google the place after my mother dies.

My brother, Charlie, and his wife, Amelia, live in western Massachusetts, but they come stay at my parents' house in Greensboro after my mom decides to stop treatment. They are quickly sucked into our myopic vortex. Charlie's working on a history PhD and Amelia is considering studying divinity, but our most animated conversations are around the topic of toothbrushing alternatives and the log of opiates. Sometimes we forget what "problem" we are solving, what enormous stillness awaits at the end.

My mom doesn't, though. Her favorite reply to any text intended to cheer her up is the Bitmoji with a hand coming out of a grave that says "Literally dying!"

Charlie is reading *The Death of Ivan Ilyich* aloud to her. She can't read books anymore by herself—pain meds, focus—but she's cognizant enough to absorb as he reads.

"Well, one thing I know is that definitely won't be me," Charlie reports that she said of Ivan Ilyich's brutal penultimate moments raging against the perceived darkness, drowning in the disbelief of life's finitude.

Charlie and I wonder about this. I mean, at one level, of course she's right: She's the opposite of Ivan Ilyich. Her life's work has been looking straight at things—including death—and she's worked on coming to terms with dying for nearly nine years.

Still: "Do you find it unsettling that Mom hasn't had more violent reactions to all of this?" Charlie texts shortly after her decision to withdraw from the endless parade of failed clinical trials.

We've both recently seen the movie *After the Wedding*, where one of the main characters—faced with a brutal diagnosis—completely loses it, sobbing and thrashing dramatically about on the floor. "Not that I wish she was, obviously, just that I'm a little suspicious of her serenity about it all," he writes.

"I know!" I write back. "Sometimes I think she's more of a Yankee than Dad."

That of course is not true. Her temper still flares from her death-bed—and her humor and her rebellious soul. The last words she speaks—several weeks from now—will be undeniably hers: *I'm so fucking fat.* But she has developed an emotional toughness to her that I find myself trying to imitate. She embodies some of that stoicism that Montaigne admired so much—a kind of fearless acceptance. Well, not fearlessness exactly—but a fearlessness of being afraid.

One morning I show up and sob in her lap. She rubs my back and looks at me sympathetically. "How are you not crying?" I ask, almost exasperated. She says, "I've done all my crying already, and I'm kind of over it. You're just a little behind."

Sunlight sneaks in through the drawn blinds and casts odd patterns on the wood floor. She asks me to bring her an ice cream sandwich and her jewelry boxes and we spend the afternoon in her bed sorting through an ancient-smelling world of gems and old chains and stories about her mother. We put all her rings on all of our fingers. She gives me a gorgeous jade pendant. "If you're ever looking for a gift for someone you don't want to spend a lot of money on, just remember this stash exists."

I ask her if there is anything she still needs to tell me about things I could be doing better, any mothering she feels has been left undone. "You are a great person in many ways," she says after a minute of thinking. "But sometimes you are too hard on people, which doesn't become you, especially when it's behind their back. And I really wish you were better about going to the dentist."

She sees visions—wispy entities whirling around her, the Pope squatting perilously on the curtain in the corner, the lilies on the mantel turning inside out to reveal their beautiful innards. She has an aura of peacefulness and grace, despite her obvious discomfort. She has moments of great clarity.

She wakes up one afternoon as I'm sitting in the chair in her room reading. "I know this song," she says to the quiet room. "It is the music of a man and a woman arguing." Then she slips back into sleep.

But, who among us is not Ivan Ilyich—absolutely creamed at times by all the missteps we have taken, stunned by where these steps have led us? Surely there must be some wild stocktaking that is still to come for her? Or is that just the work of those who love her now—to loosen our pursuit of the fox, to pull in the reins and admire the peacefulness of the forest, to be aimless in it, to stop and look up and notice the way the light filters down through the canopy?

23. *Album*

The one where she and my dad are paddling toward the Seal Rocks in the double kayak. The one where she and my aunt Francie are headed off down the path, laughing and beckoning to the photographer. The one where she's telling Charlie something important on the lawn after his wedding. The one where she's holding snoozing Benny in her lap in the Adirondack chair. The one where she and I are smiling on the porch swing. The one where she's standing on the very end of the breakwater by the boathouse—a silhouette, arms akimbo, wind whipping her hair. It is taken from a boat, and it is clear she is not greeting the photographer; she is seeing them off, although she is not waving or smiling. The tide is high, and silver waves splash the rocks. *I'm fine where I am,* her planted feet say, as if it is the end of summer and she is the only one staying behind.

STAGE THREE

1. Fifteen Signs Death Is Near

If there were an exam on the caregiver booklet that hospice gave us, titled "Fifteen Signs that Death Is Near," I feel confident that Charlie and I would both ace it.

It's almost midnight. We are sitting at the kitchen counter of our parents' house, obsessively going over the checklist that attempts to break it down by weeks, days, hours, moments. Preparing for the unpreparable. Our mom is lying on a hospital bed in a nearby room.

Her breathing pattern is changing. Check.

She hardly drinks or eats. Check.

Her extremities are cold and possibly tinged with blue. Check.

She sleeps most of the time. Check.

When she is awake, she is restless. Hallucinations are common—she may reach for things you cannot see. Yes: She seems to be working and reworking an invisible cat's cradle with her delicate bluish fingers. Or playing with Silly Putty. Or poking a hole into another dimension.

When she speaks, it is slow and difficult. She may refer to things you do not understand. "Who can trust the light?" she cries out with a start after hours of silence. Then: "Let's get out of here!"

You administer liquid morphine under her tongue from a big red bottle. Your criminal defense attorney husband assures you that you could make a fortune off it on the black market. Check.

This passes as humor. Check.

She doesn't seem to be aware of you anymore. You are beyond exhausted. Check, check.

Your dad is asleep for the first time in days in his clothes on his stomach the wrong way in the bed next to her hospital bed with the lights on. Check.

"So, what's your guess?" I ask Charlie.

"I don't know—a week, a few days?"

We both stare back into the booklet, scanning for something that is not there. Strange creatures: we who try to excel at knowing the unknowable.

Amelia, who is trained as a birth doula, seems to know better what to do. She lights candles and incense in my mom's room. She changes the water for all the cut flowers, culls the wilted ones. She rubs lotion into my mom's hands, performs some Reiki. "I'm really feeling her presence," she says at one point.

I can't feel her at all. I try to talk to her when everyone leaves the room, but I have no idea what to say. "You don't have to do this anymore," I try. She rouses and almost seems to glare at me—bewildered, annoyed. As if I would be doing this if I knew how to stop, she seems to say with her eyes.

Heartbeat and pulse may be irregular. Gurgling and conges-tion—known as the death rattle—are common and often more dis-tressing for the caregiver than uncomfortable for the patient. She may seek—or demand—"permission" to go.

Three and a half hours later, back at my house, my phone wakes me.

"I think you need to come right now," Charlie is saying.

"Why?" I ask, my brain stubbornly playing dumb. My toes grope the floor for sandals and I clip my mastectomy drain to a fresh T-shirt and I run out into the warm night.

2. What You're Afraid to Do

Back when I graduated from high school, one of my father's cousins gave me a copy of an extremely readable book of anecdotes called *Emerson in Concord*, written by my great-great grandfather about his legendary father.

One of my favorite parts is the revelation that Emerson's famous aphorism *Always do what you are afraid to do* was actually an admonition from his fierce Aunt Mary, who helped his mother raise the children after his father died when RWE was eight.

Emerson passed along this advice to his own children, and they to theirs. And here it finds me standing in my parents' doorway in Greensboro. *Walk into the house where her dead body waits. Watch your father weep.*

Enter the scene. Imagine it as your own.

3. Something New Is About to Begin

A couple hours after the sun rises on the morning she dies, we leave my mom's body on the bed in her room and go for a walk to look at St. Mary's House, the little clapboard chapel around the corner where we are thinking we'll hold the memorial service. It's an Episcopal campus ministry—and more of a cozy one-room house than a traditional church. Twelve years ago, I gave my graduate thesis poetry reading there—my parents snug on a couch watching me in the front row.

My mom left conflicting instructions on the subject of her funeral. *Do anything. Do whatever you want. Do nothing. It's not like I'm going to be there.*

Later: *Well, don't do nothing. And if you decide to toss my ashes into the ocean make sure the tide is going out, not coming in. And I'd really like Mark and Anne to sing something. And someone to say something. And, Nina, I want you to read that poem you wrote about you and me arguing in Italy.*

Even later: *Forget it. Do whatever you want. Just do something nice.*

The only thing she was consistent on: cremation. *Do not let me rot in the ground!*

I take a selfie waiting in the driveway for the others to come outside: portrait of cancer patient with dead mother. Months later, scrolling back through my pictures, right after the ones I took of her body—her anemic arms covered in deep bruises, her eerily blissful face—I discover that out of instinct I've smiled widely for the camera.

As we walk away from the house into the August morning it feels like we are passengers straggling out of the wreckage of a plane crash. We are weirdly giddy, not good company for anyone but ourselves—delirious, shattered, and still under the spell of the gallows humor we've become as dependent on as oxygen in the final weeks to stay sane.

"It's okay to leave her, right?" my dad asks.

"I think so," says Amelia. "I mean, what's the worst that could happen?"

It is the fantasy you have about your newborn after a particularly ruthless night—stepping outside, locking the door, and just walking quietly away from it all—only we actually do it.

Friday morning in late summer: School has just gone back into session, and, in the collegey neighborhood around UNC-Greensboro where my parents live, the streets are starting to fill up with students. Our awkward group ambles down the block toward the chapel. The doors of St. Mary's House are locked, but Charlie and Amelia—who have never been inside it—peer in the windows to get a sense of the space as we stand on the porch. Just then I recognize one of the backpacked students locking the door of her car and making her way toward campus—our kids' babysitter, a graduate student, who we hadn't seen in a few months since her schedule changed.

"Hey—it's Anneliesse!" I say to John. She is walking right past us, about to greet a friend on the sidewalk.

Then I realize the friend is someone we know as well—another regular babysitter, Virginia, also a grad student.

"Hey, you guys!" I am compelled to holler out. John and I walk toward them.

"Hey! Good to see you! How have you been?" All that stuff.

Charlie, Amelia, and my dad group silently behind us. What must we look like? Conspicuous. Or suspicious. Like maybe Virginia and Anneliesse are worried that the reason they haven't seen us in a while is because we've joined a cult.

"Great! Doing okay! How are you? How is the semester going so far?" It's the only thing to say.

The alternative: *I have a mastectomy drain clipped under this loose shirt. My non-hair hurts. I haven't slept in days. And my mom took her last brutal breath five hours ago. Right now she is lying by herself in her house around the corner. We're scoping out this spot here for her funeral.*

I have no idea how to introduce my family to these two young women.

"I'm sorry," I say to everyone as we walk back toward the house. "I just couldn't."

That night, Anne and Mark—two of my parents' closest friends and the ones that have possibly been conscripted to sing at the service—come over to be with us. Their daughter, Molly, is the ground zero of babysitters for us. It is through her that we know Anneliesse and Virginia.

Molly comes by the house, too, after her shift on the food truck where she's working over the summer. Anne, Amelia, Molly, and I sit and cry together with my mom's body.

"Please apologize to Anneliesse and Virginia for me?" I ask Molly, telling her about running into them. "I'm sure I was so weird."

I'm sure I was so weird—a refrain I keep repeating, mostly to myself. Because it turns out, as the days and then weeks pass, she's always right around the corner—alone in the house and newly dead. And I'm always announcing I'm okay, out here in the world where the sun is shining and something new is about to begin.

4. The Crematorium

We are following two black-suited undertakers across the one-hundred-degree parking lot out to a windowless metal building—my dad, Charlie, Amelia, me. John is at work, our kids at school. It is the day before the memorial service. My phone is buzzing in my pocket with texts of flight arrivals and last-minute arrangements.

We are all frazzled by the heat and the events of the past week, but I almost certainly look the most haggard. The hair on my head is just starting to fill in. My T-shirt sags off my body on the surgery side. I move slowly. The next three months of chemo is scheduled to start the following week.

"Dammit," my mom said a few weeks ago. "I can't believe I'm going to die right when you're in the middle of all this. It's killing me." One of her wry smiles.

The bulk of me is standing here in grief—in that unhinged and unpredictable way we are led toward things after a loss—but I have to admit that part of me is here for some kind of morbid test drive, death hitching a ride in my chest from my mom's sickbed to this parking lot behind the funeral home.

In the far back corner, in the corrugated metal building: the crematorium. *The Uglification of America*, my mom used to say when she would see this sort of cheap metal structure going up along some rural North Carolina highway, quickly announcing itself as a Dollar General or a liquor store. Now, inside one, her body awaits its final moments.

We know they'll have her in the hundred-dollar cardboard cremation casket we'd picked out at the funeral home. What we don't expect is that it will look like a large white cake box.

The morticians seem uncertain about us for wanting to be here—like it's *we* who are the creepy ones. Honestly, I'm not sure we want to be here either, but Charlie feels strongly that we should see this through to the end, and we have agreed to try to support each other through whatever twists and turns our mother's death takes us.

We kept vigil at her bedside until she died. We kept her body in the house for several days after she was gone—taking turns sitting with her, watching her change and become increasingly less her.

And now.

This is the end, I think to myself.

Three days earlier we'd sat in the funeral home office with a different mortician—our next-door neighbor, Joe, a friend and the new father of a baby girl born the week my mom died—and asked about observing the cremation.

"Uh, sure, that can definitely be arranged," Joe said. Two of his great gifts: tact and kindness.

On the glossy mahogany table in the funeral parlor was the flowered canister we'd brought from home—her stash can. "And can you put her ashes in this?" Charlie asked. "Sorry—it has kind of a strong smell. It's where she kept her pot."

"Oh, definitely," said Joe, nodding without blinking. "Not a problem."

I was actually relieved this was the container we'd shown up with. When I'd picked up my dad for the funeral home appointment, he climbed into my car holding the orange Tupperware pitcher we'd been mixing powder lemonade in since the 1970s. "Will this work?" he'd asked.

"I don't think so, Dad," I'd said. "Maybe something—not from the kitchen?"

When he ran back inside to get a different vessel, I'd snapped a photo of the pitcher sitting in the passenger seat and texted it to my mom's number. "Please come back," I'd written. "Dad wants to put you in this."

The first of a million nonreplies.

Inside the Uglification of America, it is one hundred degrees hotter than the hundred-degree parking lot. It looks like a garage, with a large cooler and even larger oven. The oven is, it seems, preheating.

"Do you want to see the body first?" one of the undertakers asks us.

She's been in their refrigerator for five days. There is a sheet covering her face when they lift the cake box lid. Of the whole thing, I like that part the least. The undertaker pulls it back with some fanfare, and the four of us lean forward and peer in at her.

She is no longer my mother—and that, I think, is part of what I'm supposed to understand by visiting her here in the metal box.

Although I knew it already. I knew it the moment my phone rang at 3:00 a.m. and Charlie said, "I think you should come," and I knew it when I skidded into the driveway and a startled rabbit in the grass by the gate stared back at me—unflinching, unmoved—as I slammed the car door and ran past it. I knew I was too late.

She isn't decomposed or anything like it, but her coloring is distinctly orange and waxy now, and her face is covered in beads of condensation. Only her hair looks like her—lovely wisps of graying brown swept back from her forehead. The purple flowers we'd strewn on her the morning she died are wilted and browning like a discarded corsage. Her eyes are sewn shut—uneven stitches between her eyelashes that look like the doll dresses she helped me sew in third grade. Her mouth is sewn shut as well.

"She would definitely not like that!" I whisper to my dad. He squeezes my shoulder.

The other undertaker turns to my dad. "Do you want to press the button for the incinerator?" he asks, as though my dad is the birthday boy at a special party. He starts showing him the levers and the different dials. My dad, who is usually game for just about anything but who I can tell in this moment is going along with the undertaker's shtick just to avoid further interaction, presses the green button.

The oven door starts to open and then lurches suddenly, and someone else's leftover ashes plume briefly into the air like a thought bubble or a dream about how little we belong here. We all jump back, and I can almost hear my mom yelling at my dad, "Jesus Christ, Peter—what are you trying to do to me?"

When the door fully opens, they close the box and slide it in on a short conveyer belt, and the oven door clanks shut with my mom inside. There is no window. Somehow all this time I had imagined there would be a horrifying little window like on a potbelly stove. There is only a thick metal door and she is on the other side of it and we cannot enter and she will not return.

The cremation itself will take four or five more hours to complete.

"Okay, I'm good," I say almost immediately. I'm light-headed and annoyed at whatever made me think this might be a reasonable thing to do. Outside, I need to squat down on my knees on the blacktop while my eyes adjust to the sun. My dad comes out with me and rubs my back. Charlie and Amelia stay inside a few minutes longer, but soon emerge.

Charlie is ten years younger than I am—my parents' second wind, a reversed vasectomy. Growing up, he and I never really fought with each other, or with our dad—it wasn't part of the architecture of our childhood—but we all fought a lot with our mom. For a long time, that was what Charlie and I had in common. Me, maybe, because I'm so much like her—impulsive, demanding, emotional. Charlie, maybe, because he is her opposite: He can be hard to connect with, and she sometimes took that personally.

"Sorry about that," says Charlie, cry-laughing, Amelia leaning her head against him as we all walk arm-in-arm back to the car. "I don't know if that was okay or horrible."

"It was okay," says my dad. "Let's just not ever do it again."

After the cremation the rest of the afternoon is airport runs and phone calls, and the evening is soup and beers on the back patio with music and family and friends. An old best friend pulls into the driveway on her motorcycle, driven that day from New York. Amelia's parents are here. John's mom and sister have both flown in from out West. They walk through the gate. The neighbors bring dessert. All through this, the oven is at work in the back of that parking lot on the other side of town.

We hold two services. The first one is at tiny St. Mary's House, where my parents' and my friends all sit packed in a giant circle and look at each other, crying and smiling. The kids sit on pillows on the floor and form an impromptu band with a few of their friends to help Mark get through his beautiful rendition of an Everybodyfields song—"By Your Side"—on the guitar. They play harmonica and bongos and beat the wooden floor with their hands. They are exceptionally pleased with themselves.

I've asked people to wear bright colors if they want because my mom loved bright clothes. Her favorite color was purple, although three days before she died she changed it to orange.

"Orange," she kept telling my dad. "Orange is the best."

"You want to eat an orange?" my dad would reply, always trying to feed her.

"No," she would shake her head fiercely. "I love orange."

Two nights before she died she had a nightmare that she was

going to be abducted. She woke up agitated, restless, panicky. She couldn't escape the dream world. Ativan didn't work. Neither did the pain pills. "Let's just think about orange," my dad eventually tried. "Meditate on orange." He rubbed her feet and talked her through every orange thought he could generate at 3:00 a.m. Finally, her breathing calmed and she slept again.

A friend tells me that this is significant: In Buddhism, orange is considered to be a highly evolved color, representing illumination (*who can trust the light?!*) and essence—something full of wisdom, strength, and dignity.

I love that she could go her whole life ardently loving purple, and then shift to an equally passionate affinity for orange less than a week before she died. It's exactly like her: She had strong opinions but was never afraid to change them—to evolve or retract or alter. Her favorite way to start a sentence—"You know what your problem is?"—was closely rivaled by "You know what I was wrong about?"

After the songs, Charlie reads a poem. Friends share memories. My dad—not one for public speaking—grips my hand as we sit on the chapel's cozy couch.

I apologize for not reading the poem she asked me to about Italy—I just can't do it. I fail to follow Emerson's Aunt Mary's advice. And because I can't stand seeing people feel unhappy, I tell silly slapstick stories that she loved to tell: the way she was a magnet for the ridiculous, the time she got stuck on an airplane toilet, the time the bumblebee flew up her nose, the time she was scooping up dog poop and it ended up in her hair, the time in San Francisco that she had gone pantie-less to the bank when I was a baby and she set me down on the floor while she filled out a form and I pulled her hippy skirt down to her ankles and wouldn't let go. I feel her voice in my mouth.

As I'm talking, a picture of the Virgin Mary hanging behind me suddenly falls off the wall and crashes to the floor. Lots of gasps and some laughter. "Jeez, Jan," someone says. "Give it a rest already."

We end the service with an open-ended moment of silence. We tell people they are free to go whenever they want. Before the memorial, when we were planning this, I kept worrying that people would feel awkward or uncertain or like they needed to stay as long as others do. I wanted there to be a gong or bell at the end of the moment to let people know it was okay to go.

Charlie was clearer: "It's about honoring the unknowing and the awkwardness and the mystery of dying," he said. "It's unsettling—and that's okay."

Oh my God, I thought. *I am terrible at death. I don't know how any of this is supposed to work at all.*

It will be a couple days before we receive the ashes from the cremation because, as Joe the mortician tells me one morning in the driveway, after the incinerator, there is the cremulator—a high-speed blender of sorts that grinds the cremated bone fragments into approximately four pounds of rocky sand.

Two days after the memorial service, Joe rings the doorbell holding the stash can. He's home from work for a quick lunch, the hearse crowding the narrow driveway between our houses. His wife, Josie, is home full-time with the baby, and Joe is trying to get back to working a regular schedule. His eyes are raw with the shock of parenting. I can hear the sound of newborn cries through our open windows at all hours.

"These are for you," he says when I open the door, handing me the container. Four pounds.

"Thank you," I say, holding it awkwardly with both hands, wanting to put it under my arm, but knowing that would not be right either. "I hope you guys are doing okay over there."

"We are," he says, smiling. "Tired—but she's so great."

Fifteen minutes later I peer out the dining room window. The driveway is empty. I discover I'm still holding the canister, balanced on my hip and in the crook of my arm. I've let the dog out and straightened the couch cushions and made a grocery list, but I haven't put it down. Through the screens, I can hear Josie humming and cooing to the baby—that mindless meandering tune of comfort and companionship—the loveliest of music, one of the first sounds I imagine I ever heard.

5. Plunder

One afternoon, I stop by my parents' house to drop off some papers for my dad, who has gone back to work. My mom's Prius is in the driveway. Her purse is hanging on the chair in the kitchen.

Oh, good, I have to stop myself from thinking, *she's home.*

Their ancient beagle, Clyde, is sprawled snoring in the hall and does not look up. The house is hushed and glowing with afternoon sun, an orchid blooming on the dining room table. Everything seems as it should be. I walk into her bedroom.

Seems—such a sneaky word.

In the days right after she died, her bedroom smelled like, well—death. We all noticed it. Not an outright bad smell, but kind of a cocktail of all the smells of those final weeks and days and hours. Lotions, Clorox, incense, medicine, flowers, breath. Plus something else. Decay, I guess. The scent was in my nose for days.

She died in bed around four in the morning on Friday, and we kept her body there all through the next day and into midmorning on Sunday. Hospice came around dawn on Friday to help us clean her and dress her—we opened the blinds and blasted the Beatles and put her in the funkiest outfit and covered her in purple flowers. She looked radiant. She would have swooned over the luminance of her skin.

Something I didn't expect: She didn't leave all at once. And I don't really mean that in an esoteric way at all. At first she was present, even though she was lifeless. But every time I would go into and out of her room, I would come back to something newly less "there." The way her fingers were curled on her chest (those softest, most delicate hands—my earliest memory), her lips, the color of her skin. By Sunday morning it was her eyes—they'd changed to a vinyl-looking film; they were not hers at all.

The same thing has happened with the death smell. When I walk in the bedroom, it is pristine—much as she kept it before she was sick enough to relinquish those duties to us. The cleaning lady has come. The marigold-print bedspread is crisp and fresh and square, her unguents are neatly aligned on the nightstand next to her glasses and her green comb, and her orderly stacks of camisoles and yoga pants all smell of fresh detergent.

I walk around the room twice, sniffing at everything—searching for just one whiff of her—organic, living/dying her. It is not here. So I stand in the room and cry for a long time.

And then I steal all her shoes.

I don't really know what comes over me. It started happening even before she died, after she stopped being able to walk. I would go over to hang out and while she was dozing I'd poke around in her closet and try on sandals and boots and clogs I'd never given two thoughts to before. And then I'd leave with a pair.

She's about a half size smaller than me—and we don't even totally align in terms of taste—but I can't stop myself. I pile all her shoes into a big shopping bag and lug them to my house. And now I'm in my bedroom scrunching up my toes and tromping around in them.

6. Red Devil

The kids are deeply annoyed that I'm headed back into chemo. They hate it when I'm not there to pick them up from school, to schlep to piano lessons and swimming, to pack their snacks, help plan their class parties. And I appreciate that their enormous self-centeredness is still intact.

"Didn't they do a lot of chemo already?" Freddy asks at supper. "What kind is this one?"

"It's called Adriamycin," I say. "It's bright red. Like as red as Kool-Aid. The nurses called it the Red Devil."

"We'll bring some home for you as a treat," says John.

"No thank you," says Benny with genuine indignance.

I tell the boys it won't be much different from the last time.

"But this time you have to do it without your mom," Freddy points out. "I would hate that."

"It's okay," I say. "I have you guys. Seems like given all your super powers and epic warfare strategies, you might be able to help me with the Red Devil."

"The problem is they're lazy," says John. "They're only interested in vanquishing evil when they're in the right mood."

"Totally," I say.

That night John finds the boys asleep with the lights on in their bunk. Freddy has been drawing a comic book: Red Devil vs. the Cell Creep. You know the tale.

7. Labor Day

The second service is to scatter the ashes. Labor Day: We drive up to our family place on the Cape. Dozens of cousins and aunts and uncles. The landscape of vacation. The boys are thrilled to miss school, extend the summer a few more days. The hill is turning brown, the corners of the island are sharpened, the ocean has shifted from hazy gray-green to chilly navy.

I feel the future coming like a promise: motherless September, more chemo, and after that—whatever it is that happens when the doctors set you adrift on the sea of *after treatment*.

I sit on the porch swing before the ceremony and watch a guinea hen nervously pecking around in the lawn with her head bobbing up and down in the grass—a vigilant look to the task at her feet, another to the horizon, and again—and I understand what it is to dawdle in the sun on a perfect day and feel winter and grief in the warm breeze and in the dry rustle of the grasses and in the waves in the bay newly tipped with white.

We had started the season with a flock of eight guinea hens— exotic-looking, high-strung, speckled fowl known for eating ticks, which infest the island. Beautiful, anxious birds. They roamed free around the yard during the day, laying eggs, disappearing together into the tall grasses, squabbling, munching on ticks and other bugs, and periodically working themselves into loud, seemingly unprovoked lathers.

"Oh chill out, ladies," we'd say when they would abruptly round a corner and zigzag madly across the lawn in a frantic rush toward nothing and away from nothing. They seemed to work each other up like a pack of kids telling ghost stories. "You're fine, birdies. No worries."

At night they were cooped and quiet—safe from the coyotes that prowl and yip along the island beaches after dark—in a henhouse perched on the cliff near the ice-age boulder and the clothesline where even before my mom died I could sometimes feel her ghost and the outdoor shower with its mermaid mural and front-row view of fishing boats and sailboats and ferries shuttling vacationers out to the Vineyard.

Early in the summer, the guineas made a nest in a thicket of poison ivy just off the road down to the barn, and we discovered they must not have all been hens one day when, after a great deal of squawking and fluttering, suddenly there was a collection of downy chicks huddled on the path.

One was dead or nearly dead. The others were not yet very mobile, and all day the kids ran up and back reporting on the status of the babies and arguing over their names and personality traits—getting as close as the alarmist flock would permit before they would flap up and dive at the boys' heads. Then, on one visit, the ruckus turned to something more serious, squawks turning to sirens, and the boys watched an osprey swoop down out of the sky and carry off one of the chicks—Clarence or Roberto or FuzzWuzz—and the boys began screeching and flapping themselves.

And then again, minutes later, after the grown-ups had been

pulled into the unfolding crisis, the osprey returned and snatched another. And then another.

We yelled at the sky, "*Stop that right now!*" and the guineas all shrieked and the boys shook sticks in the air and the osprey with the chick in its grip looped up and out, disappearing over the hill and the gray-green waves, silent and unmoved as a paper airplane, and when, despite our efforts, every last chick was gone, we walked back to the house to explain with uncertainty in our throats about the cycle of life.

We felt more tolerant of the guineas' excitability after that— more of a kinship with their constant fretting. When one or two of them would get separated from the group and start to squawk, we'd say, "Hang on, you'll find them in a minute," and we'd crane our necks around until we spotted the flock pecking their way up the path from the boathouse or emerging from under the porch.

Over the course of the summer, they disappeared one by one— the occasional catastrophe of dark-gray speckled feathers in the grass. We'd lost other guinea hens in seasons past, but never at this rate. The flock began to stick closer together; they were more rattled, shriller—if possible. We'd count them each night and felt relief when they all were tucked in their roost and the door closed. When we were down to one, my uncle found a fox den nestled in the cliff about seventy-five feet from the henhouse.

The final guinea hen. She busies herself under the porch and along the path during the day. She weaves in and out of the grasses.

She does not stop moving until she returns to the roost on her own before dusk each evening. It seems it is not easy to find peace as the last living member of your species at the end of summer on an island in the chilly Atlantic. What must she be thinking? There is no fear as great as her fear. From time to time she lets loose a great squawk, standing at the highest spot on the hill—a desperate hollow call out into a world where the wind blows and the sun shines and children and dogs run in the lawn but where there is no one that matters to answer.

As I watch her I remember a dream I've had that I am alone in a white empty room. I can hear Freddy and Benny talking, then arguing, and one of them starts to cry. But I can't see them anywhere, and I cannot say a thing.

At noon, maybe sixty members of my dad's expansive family—the family that has over the years become my mom's family and many of her most beloved people—gather at her favorite spot by the flagpole, the spot where I like to picture her in the Adirondack chair, chatting with her sisters-in-law and gazing out at the water and laughing.

It's breezy and sunny up on the hill. We break flag protocol—which requires an act of Congress or presidential decree to fly a flag at half-mast—at the request of Freddy and Benny. It's not the kind of thing my grandfather would have ever permitted, but: Times have changed. Once, in 1974—on my mom's first visit to the Cape on a trip back East from San Francisco—my grandparents still vibrant and in charge—after a family picnic on horseback down island and a vigorous trail-clearing expedition (known affectionately as a "chopping party"), everyone had gathered in the living room for cocktails. My grandfather was storytelling and holding forth as he loved to do: Harvard pranks, rowing regattas, feats of physical prowess, women he'd charmed.

My mother, sitting on a lumpy cushion stuffed with horsehair next to the enormous picture window that gapes out at the water and the old-money mansions that line Vineyard Sound, looked around the room, set down her drink on the wooden chest that belonged to Ralph Waldo Emerson's grandson, pulled out a cigarette and a match, lit up, and took the universe's longest drag. I believe she relished the silence in the room and the shock on my grandfather's face for forty years. The slightest smirk on RWE's face in the portrait over the mantel suggests that the Concord Sage himself has still not recovered. *Always do what you are afraid to do.*

My dad, the youngest and least assuming in a family of five other boys and a girl, had found his ticket. He didn't know whether he wanted to disappear or celebrate, but he knew he was home — at last — with her.

He is standing next to me at the pole. I can feel him trembling. He whispers *thank you* to me — for doing the planning I guess, maybe for still being here. I have my hands on the shoulders of Freddy and Benny, who are wiggling with excitement at being the center of attention. John has his hand on the small of my back. In our ways, we hold each other upright.

First my dad, then Charlie and I, take handfuls of her ashes and face the ocean and offer them up to the breeze. Freddy winds up and pretends to throw a fastball with his. A slow procession from the crowd takes their turns. We watch each one. The wind is such that for a moment each handful hangs in the air like a beautiful specter contemplating our group—nearly returning to us, then spirited away, sometimes almost a recognizable shape, sometimes something entirely unfamiliar.

8. Summer House

Here is the summer house—the picnic dishes, the drawer of dull knives, the white sheets on the line that work the air of the cooler days like sails, like lost souls, like wings that need more imagining, filling the yard—huffing and brimming.

Here are the seventy-year-old antlers, the glass buoys, the miniature cairns of white pebbles, yellowed paperbacks, checkers, frayed semaphore flags, the tightly furled nests in the eaves of barn swallows.

Here is the swallow herself—swooping, whirling, screeching—frantic to return to her four wet beaks.

Here is the path to the gravestone like a trick map, like a prank, like an incomplete thought. Here the dip in the lawn where the groom found the bride, here the fever of remembering, here the work we do that we love to do.

Here lay my baby in my mother's lap, drifting through his dream of the whine of an outboard. Here on the porch, the sweet globe of a plum. Here the tooth that pierces the peel like a door burst open, like a flood, like an afterlife.

Here are the children engulfing the house in a game of sardines, each one tucked tighter into the pooled dark of the closet until a single child is left to enter the room calling out, sensing in the hush that the rest have found each other—her hand lingering on the doorknob.

9. Reconstruction

Ginny writes: "It's such bullshit that there are plenty of Joan Crawfords and assholes like my husband running around among us and your mom is not."

She lost her dad a few years back—suicide. She knows what to say and what not to say. "We threw my sweet dad into the Beaufort River with three ospreys flying over (he loved ospreys because the daddies take care of the babies). There is something awesome about returning them to the earth."

Her breast reconstruction has gone terribly wrong in the non-cancer breast that they took off for good measure. An infection. The doctors have had to tear out the implant until things settle down and they can try again. For now we are both just two left boobs—mine real and hers fake.

"My mom's death feels exactly like this wound on my chest," I text her. "Sometimes I get confused about which pain I'm feeling."

"I know," she says. "Me, too."

10. Red Face

Another thing I've spirited from my mom's possessions is her blue cruiser bike. My dad tunes it all up for me, and it fits me really nicely, unlike her Tevas.

With the chemo, I'm back on the steroids. Before the kids get home from school, I fly down the hill on Mendenhall Street all wild and nonbraking. I zip along the greenway, bugs flying into my mouth, and realize I am both laughing out loud and completely out of breath.

On the way home, I have to walk the bike up the Mendenhall hill. I pass a neighbor walking his dog who stares blankly at me and my heart-attack face after I say, "Hey! How are you?" until I gulp, "Nina! The green house with the red door! Breast cancer!" Why do I say that last part?

It registers. "Oh hi," he says, "Are you okay?"

First of all—*Ha. Yes. Totally.*

Second of all, *I do not know.* I wish there was someone else we could ask.

11. The Ache

Right before all your hair falls out, it aches. Like a ponytail pulled back for too long. And even after it's all gone, the ache resurfaces. You run your hands through the air, but assuage nothing.

John and I get a babysitter so we can join Mark, Anne, and my dad at the bar the first Friday after the memorials. I sit in the car for several minutes before we go in, trying to shake loose the hairs that have already let go. I am noticeably patchier when we sit down at the table than when we left the house. I am fighting enormous tears and Anne reaches out and squeezes my hand and asks how I'm feeling. Mark says, "This is not fair."

My parents and Mark and Anne had a standing Friday night date—almost up to the end. When she was too unwell to go out, my mom and Anne would hang out in the salon while Mark and my dad went to the corner bar. Then, blood full of cocktails, they would all reconvene for food—sometimes around my mom's bedside—where'd she'd be sipping a gin and tonic and they'd all be laughing their heads off and telling dirty jokes and sometimes singing and playing music until past their bedtime.

My mother was the queen of dirty jokes, mortifying Charlie and me from middle school into adulthood. *How do you make a woman scream twice? What did the pilot say to the stewardess?* She had predictably poor timing and a knack for fumbling the punch line, which made the jokes far funnier than they normally would be.

I'm sitting next to my Dad at the bar. I am a B-list stand-in for my mother, who would never be crying like this. Who would be making this whole table laugh as the cancer gnawed on her bones.

12. *The Little Brick House*

We return to Massachusetts for a family wedding a month into the latest chemo. We leave the kids at home with friends. I shave my head tidily. I go bald-headed to the rehearsal dinner. My aunt Cami, who has gone two rounds with breast cancer, takes me in her arms and sways with me for a moment.

We stay with my Emerson cousins in Concord. Their house is just a brisk walk through the Estabrook Woods away from where we lived when I was young, long before Charlie was born, in the tiny brick cottage on my great-grandparents' estate. Past Punkatasset Hill, the sledding hill, and Hutchins Pond. Past the ghostly stand of white birches. Across the meadow and up along the fire road. My cousins lived in my dead great-grandparents' house across the field, and more cousins lived in a house just down the road.

The estate was sold decades ago to a family with the money to keep it up: Fancy stables now sprawl over the site of the old barn and an immaculately shingled farmhouse stands where my great-grandparents' rambling homestead once stood—a grand but unsettling house with three stories and back stairways and a ghost named Mr. Dutton. The old driveway where my cousins and I learned to ride our bikes has been regraded as a gentler slope— almost like a trick of memory. But the little brick house still stands on the far side of the field.

It is much quainter than it used to be—a rose-covered trellis, a picket fence around the perimeter, dormers, a bright blue door—but completely recognizable. John and I walk toward it along the fire road. The house appears to be empty.

My mother often described the time we lived here as the happiest in her life, which is odd, considering she—born and raised in Panama—was transplanted here into the Yankee den from California for the snowiest winter in years. That year—the winter of 1981—snow fell through April in impossibly huge, magical piles that my mother and I had never dreamed of. One November morning when I was four, while I was sleeping in a makeshift bed of blankets by the back door while my dad built a stairway up to the attic—which was being converted into my bedroom—I woke up under a drift of snow from a blizzard that had blown the door open in the night. I remember my toes cold and wet, thawing between my parents' warm, sleepy bodies when I scrambled into their bed.

My father taught my mom and me to cross-country ski, and we would clamp on our skis sitting on the back stoop and disappear within minutes into the silence of the Estabrook Woods. Even by age five, I understood that this life was unsustainably simple. If you wandered into the barn you would find: chickens, an uncle tinkering with a tractor engine, a half-built kite, the echo of my dad chopping wood across the field. Once, I remember hearing screaming and then laughter as my cousin Bonnie and I dug holes in the yard by the brick house. It came from our mothers in the garden. Mine had stepped on a garter snake and it had bitten her. "You are brave," I remember saying to her as she iced her ankle in the kitchen while cleaning lettuce. "I can't believe you survived a snakebite!"

The earliest seeds of anxiety: I am lying in bed in the attic on the night before the first day of kindergarten, afraid to roll over, afraid to breathe deeply—for fear that I will miss the first crackle, the first hint of smoke from a fire that could burn our house to the ground and keep me from ever becoming a kindergartener or being able to wear the new red turtleneck and tan corduroy skirt that matches Bonnie's, laid out on my dresser for morning.

In two years, my grandparents' bodies will be filling with cancer. The grown-ups will be older and thinking about careers and next steps and houses of their own. The houses at Estabrook Woods will need to be sold or repaired. My mother will have grown to despise winter—its isolation, its piles of coats, its metaphorical kinship with the Yankee heart.

"Talking to you about your feelings is like sliding down an icy road," she will say to my dad. "Sounds kinda fun," my dad will say. They will slip and spin out and glide and slip again for the next thirty-five years.

"Will you take a picture of me here by the steps?" I ask John as we prowl around toward the stoop of the empty brick house where I remember, with Bonnie, burying a cereal bowl in the dirt that we hope anthropologists will discover thousands of years from now as a key to civilization.

I adjust my chemo cap.

✳   ✳   ✳

"Life is a progress, and not a station," says my great-great-great grandfather Emerson. In 1837, forty five years before he died in his house down the road in town, he also wrote this in his journal:

> I said when I awoke, After some more sleepings and wakings I shall lie on this mattress sick; then, dead; and through my gay entry they will carry these bones. Where shall I be then? I lifted my head and beheld the spotless orange light of the morning beaming up from the dark hills into the wide Universe.

Orange. "Did you think you would never reach the point toward which you were constantly heading?" asks Montaigne.

13. Kind of Blue

John is on a mission to complicate things with something that can fetch. "What about this guy?" reads his fifth email of the morning containing a link from petfinder.com. "He loves brisk walks and kids. He's recovering from a scrotal infection and likes to dig but otherwise he's perfect!"

I guess I'm not exactly dissuading him from his search. I'm in the market for something to hold and snuggle these days. Ellie, our old black mutt, is not a snuggler.

So we drive to Charlottesville—three hours—to adopt Blue, an Australian cattle dog.

I love Route 29 as it climbs up Virginia. The uncrowded lanes and all the roadside family restaurants and sleepy service stations and the tiny towns of Hurt and Tightsqueeze. The aboveground pool dealers and shed dealers and dump truck dealers. The sprawling ranch partially remodeled as a Monticello replica and all the crosses and the Dairy Queens.

The boys want to give Blue a new name. From the backseat, for the whole ride there: *Can we call him Maverick? Can we call him Sheriff? Can we call him Alberto? Can we call him Obsidian?*

The whole trip home I ride in the way back with the new dog in my lap licking my face. I don't notice the three hours because I am very busy falling in love with his crazy black belly spots and what Freddy called his "boyish eyes" and his coy, smart face. He licks the boys' ears from behind them and makes them laugh. He obsessively watches every single person come out of a gas station and when it is finally John he starts to whine and wiggle with excitement like he's known him for years.

I can't stop smiling at John when our eyes meet in the rearview mirror. "How about Pancho," he says somewhere near Lynchburg—and that seems just right.

"Pancho. You're Pancho," I whisper to the dog. "And you're in our family."

Everyone is happy. Well, everyone except Ellie. She is having a quiet, protracted nervous breakdown on the floor behind the driver's seat.

What started out as the dogs seeming a little standoffish to each other when they first met in Charlottesville devolves into full-on mortal enmity after about twenty-four hours at home. They can't be in a room together. Blue/Pancho snaps and bullies. Ellie quakes and hides. We catch Ellie trying to dig out of her own backyard.

We speak to a dog behaviorist on the second morning. "I can fix this," she says, "but it won't be easy. And in the end it may not be the right thing for either dog. If it were me, I'd take him back. There are lots of great rescue dogs in the world. You need to find the right one for everyone in your family."

The sadness of the boys, who have been conspiring about how to rig up a ramp so the dog can sleep in their top bunk, is big. After we break the news, they take Blue/Pancho out in the yard and the three of them play basketball together for almost an hour—

Freddy shooting baskets, Benny running around kicking leaves off the court, the dog leaping into the air to rebound the ball. I video the whole thing on my phone and keep it there, just to make it even worse.

Blue and I leave for Charlottesville on our own right after John takes the boys off to school the next day. Ellie won't even come out from her new bunker under the chair in the bedroom to pee.

We listen to NPR and Paul Simon the whole way because no one is there to tell us not to. Blue loves "Under African Skies" but is exasperated by the lack of clarity from the Dutch report on the Malaysian plane shot down last year over Ukraine.

He sniffs the Virginia morning vigorously through the window crack, then groans a little and falls asleep with his head on my thigh and his body sprawling awkwardly over the gearbox and into the passenger seat.

What is the opposite of a sleeping dog's head in your lap while you drive?

The ride home is the slowest of the four trips. I mostly think about work and to-do lists. I cry a little. The next day I'm due at Duke to meet my radiation oncologist and talk about the next phase of treatment so I also think about tumors and cancer cells and what the hell the doctors say to you if they do all the things they know how to do and there is still cancer left.

And I think: *Right now, this is grieving.* My mom feels a million miles away and that distance is permanent and inexplicable and I'm so tired of feeling scared and losing things. I think about why, one day when all my hair was falling out this time around, I was compelled to rewrite the last paragraph of Joyce's "The Dead" by replacing snow with hair:

It had begun to fall again. She watched listlessly the hair, silver and brown, falling obliquely against the lamplight. . . . It was falling, too, upon every part of the bed sheets and the bathroom floor. It lay thickly drifted in the sink basin and shower drain, between the wooden floorboards, on the hand soap. Her soul swooned slowly as she heard the hair falling faintly through the universe and faintly falling, like the descent of their last end, upon all the living and the dead.

That was grief, I say to myself. *It makes us dark and a little crazy.*

By then, I am pulling back into Greensboro, and instead of going home I head straight to Target because buying poster board for Freddy's social studies project about Panama is on my to-do list. There, I promptly lose one more thing: my purse—with an unusually flush amount of cash stuffed in my wallet due to selling my inherited dining room table on craigslist on a whim (*dark and crazy,* I tell you)—left in the shopping cart in the parking lot.

I realize it halfway home and drive like a maniac back up Battleground Avenue. It isn't in the cart, still wedged in the return enclosure. I look back through my car—it definitely isn't there. I walk into the store and must be staring wildly at the security guard because she immediately walks over to me and says sternly, "Ma'am, is there something we can help you with?"

They have it. Someone has just turned it in—an older woman who is in fact still standing there. I can tell by the look on her face she has clearly seen all the cash. "You're very lucky it was me who found it," she whispers. "You could have just had a very bad day."

As I am walking back to the car, a text pings in from inside my purse. John.

"Are you back yet? You have to check out this one. He's smart and low-key and gets along well with other dogs. Plus look at those ears!"

And there I am—because this is just what we do—sitting in the Target parking lot, door still open, clicking on the link.

14. Redemption

John eventually finds "the one" at a rescue shelter down in Mocksville, about an hour from Greensboro. He is a ridiculous mix of corgi and collie and in his Internet pictures he looks like someone Photoshopped his huge, black, luck-dragon head onto his short, white body. His name is Azoo. John, the kids, my dad, and I all squish into the car and drive to the shelter on a school night after John and my dad get off work. The kids keep howling "Azooooooo!" Ellie is quivering in the backseat, still traumatized from Blue.

We are led into an unmarked warehouse carpeted with Astroturf and lined with secondhand church pews by a man named Tony who tells us to sit still and silently while he unloads dog crates from his pickup truck. Tony, close to seven feet tall with an unusual paramilitary/hippy vibe, appears to be more of a curator of dogs than shelter operator.

"I've brought three dogs here tonight," he says, pacing in front of us on the Astroturf. "One is Azoo, who you requested. The other is Jordan—the collie mix you also expressed interest in. The third is an unknown. He's brand-new to my farm and not on the website, but I thought I'd bring him along just in case. I will take them out one by one for you and Ellie to meet. I will ask you to keep your sons from making sudden movements until the dogs are at ease in the room."

Ellie is curled up under the church pew, panting like a madwoman.

We love Azoo—he's as fantastically patchwork in person as in his pictures—and Ellie loves Azoo and Azoo loves Ellie. But Azoo quivers and yips and hides between Tony's legs whenever the kids come near. "I think Azoo might need a lower energy household," says Tony.

Jordan enters the room like a racquetball—bouncing off the walls and the pews, into my dad's lap, over the small barrier by the door. The kids can't stop giggling. Ellie shakes in the corner, pees a little.

When the mystery dog comes out, I am sitting cross-legged on the floor with Benny in my lap. He sniffs us and promptly plops into our pile. Ellie comes over to give him a sniff, wags her tail. He's so shaggy he looks like a Muppet—or like he's wearing footie pajamas made to look like a dog costume. "I don't know," says Tony. "Something about this guy just speaks to me for you all."

After cuddling him for fifteen minutes, I struggle to get off the floor—I'm in my last cycle of chemo and my body aches and my back has been bothering me on and off. My dad gives me a hand and the Muppet lies down on top of my feet. The kids nuzzle his belly. John and I exchange hopeful looks.

"I noticed your head," says Tony, addressing me directly for the first time. "You look like my wife. Ovarian cancer. It's been one hell of a year. Almost lost her a couple weeks ago."

He tells me their dog is responsible for finding the cancer. "Wouldn't stop sniffing this spot in her abdomen. One day, he almost attacked her there—leaping on her and punching her with his nose—and she ended up in the hospital. Sure enough, doctors found a tumor the size of a grapefruit."

"Amazing," I say. "Dogs sure know how to take care of us when we need it."

"I think you all found the right one," says Tony. The Muppet and Ellie are sniffing something together under one of the pews. We adopt him.

We discuss names that night on the drive home. I want to call him Montaigne.

"Let's not be assholes," says John. We settle on MacDuff.

15. *Twilight Zone*

One Saturday afternoon in fall, my dad pulls into our driveway on a red and black motorcycle. I'm standing in the yard and I don't realize it's him at first with his helmet on.

"I did it," he says, taking the helmet off but making no move to get off the bike. He's bought it from a retired cop out in the county. It's a Honda Shadow, in beautiful shape, and it comes with gear—luggage and chaps and gloves and multiple helmets. I can tell right away this must have been a death pact with my mom: "Over my dead body," she must have said. "Okay," he must have agreed.

"Want a ride?" he asks.

I hoist myself onto the back and put my arms around his waist and we head straight north out of town, up past the old defunct Revolution Mill and toward the windier roads that snake through the northern reaches of Guilford County. I rest my helmeted head on his back and feel the sun warming my arms and legs. My body feels young and someone is burning leaves in their yard and the rumble of the engine means there is no need to talk. *Grief,* I think. *Sometimes it is* not *dark* or *crazy*. On the way back into town we pass the hospice building, where several weeks after my mom died my dad and I sat together in stiff upholstered chairs crying to a twentysomething-year-old grief counselor with a handshake like a silk scarf to whom we'd been referred after my mom's death.

My dad told her he'd been binge watching old *Twilight Zone* episodes.

"Sometimes it's a little much," he said. "Like I can't tell what's real and what's on TV."

"I can totally see that," I remember she said. "Maybe just don't watch so many episodes at a time? But otherwise, it's normal. That's what I like to remind people. Everything you're feeling is completely normal."

16. Symmetry

Dr. Cavanaugh doesn't want me to have breast reconstruction at all.

"That's a survivor issue," she tells me. "We're not there yet. And I don't want your immune system focused on anything except fighting cancer."

It makes sense, but I really miss being symmetrical sometimes. I stuff my bra with a little breast-shaped hand-sewn cushion that Benny dubs the Pink Critter when he sees it sitting on my dresser.

Pink Critter is lumpy and prone to awkward bulging, though. And then one day MacDuff hops up on our bed illicitly, finds Pink Critter there, and devours it—just a few pieces of wet batting left in the hallway as evidence.

Benny is devastated: "Poor Critter! He was so soft and useful! I'll never forgive that dog!"

John calls a dog trainer and I call Dr. Cavanaugh's nurse to ask for a more permanent solution—maybe something MacDuff will be less inclined to eat. Dr. Cavanaugh writes me a prescription for a breast prosthetic and tells me to go talk to Alethia in the gift shop down on Level 0 of the cancer center.

Tita comes with me. We find Alethia not so much *in* the gift shop, but in a windowless room *behind* the gift shop—a room of her own stacked with boxes, file cabinets, racks of specialty bras of all shapes and sizes and materials, and drawers upon drawers of breast "forms." All the bras have sewn-in pockets where you can insert a breast form on either or both sides.

Alethia greets us like she's been expecting us for a lifetime, hugging us both to her own bosom—by far the most impressive breast-related item in the room.

"Welcome!" she says. "Let's find you a breast!"

She tells me that according to my insurance, I get to pick out six bras and a breast form. Black, white, beige—easy. A strapless. A sports bra.

"Do you want something lacy and sexy?" Tita asks. I think about John's gaze falling on me, undressed. My body. My carved up, asymmetrical body.

"No," I say. "Not really."

I choose a second black bra, with a small bow and the slightest sheen.

For the breast forms, we poke our fingers into different degrees of density, different shapes. They all feel like something between a memory foam pillow and a balloon.

"The new ones are waterproof," says Alethia as we browse. "And really keep their shape nicely."

We are giggling and cupping them in our hands. We have no idea what to pick, what the best option is to get the right curve. I ask Alethia to choose for me. The one she picks comes in a fancy square box with gold embossed writing: Nearly Me.

"That one is made by the lady who invented Barbie," Alethia tells us.

"Well, then that's a done deal," says Tita.

At home I model my new breast and bras under a tight T-shirt for John.

"What do you think of my optical illusion?" I ask. "The Amazing Appearing Woman."

"Lovely," he says. "But I still prefer you topless, even when you're lopsided."

"Aww," I say. "Liar."

I agree with him though. I appreciate having the ability to suggest symmetry, but sometimes I prefer the one-sidedness, the wrongness of it—the gap and the scar. It's a truth, an artifact—a way to put my hands on my losses and take stock.

17. *Not Men-o'-War*

First major holiday after my mom dies, and we rent a beach house down on the coast. I wake and cook the pies early. My dad and John tend the turkey. The beach is deserted, except by sunlight and crab carcasses. The boys run until they cannot.

One morning we wake to a line of jellyfish rolling aimlessly in the surf for as long as the eye can see. Not men-o'-war, but not clear and harmless either.

"I know they're kind of creepy, but I like them," says Freddy, poking one with a stick. "The way they allow themselves to be swept this way and that. Like they're always up for a new adventure."

"I like how you can see their nice red hearts from the outside," says Benny.

"Those aren't their hearts, Benny! Jeez!" corrects Freddy. "Those are their stingers!"

"Oh," says Benny. "Well, that way they can not get hurt as much on their adventure."

Here we are closer to something I am trying to understand: that openness to fear. We are hearts and stingers. We ride the tide. We believe in resistance; we are made both of fight and float.

Freddy and I take sticks and write in the wet sand thanks to things we admit have made us stronger, but are ready to say goodbye to: CANCER and DIABETES. Then we stand and watch it wash away on the rising tide. Benny chooses to write POOP.

"What?" he says with one of his grins. "It's good to say thanks and goodbye to poop, too."

18. The Machine

Radiation is daily for a month—I start after Thanksgiving and am supposed to be done by Christmas. Freddy—who loves to stay up late reading about atoms and quarks—has been unfortunately stuck on the notion of being a Billionaire Weapons Inventor for a while now. And Benny has an entire notebook of recipes he's conjured for how to turn humans into different animal species (tail hair of a Welsh corgi, saliva of an ocelot, chocolate chips, sea salt). Nudging them away from the realm of evil science toward the realm of medical science seems like it can't hurt, and might possibly be at least as lucrative someday in their future, so I decide to bring them to see the machine.

My radiation oncologist Dr. Rosenblum—who has a little boy— thinks it's a great idea.

"Make sure to tell your boys the machine is called a 'linear accelerator,'" she tells John and me at the appointment before I start radiation.

"Ooh—and wait—how old are they again? Eight and six? Yeah, tell them we'll be using lasers to guide the photons and electrons to the right spot and that we will be using the exact same technology we use for radar. And that we will do it all from a remote command center with closed-circuit monitors! And that each machine costs millions of dollars!"

Her eyes are glowing maybe a little too brightly.

I mention all this at the dinner table that night as casually as possible.

"Hmmm," says Freddy, a little interested. "What are the chances you'll come away from this with mutant powers?"

"I imagine not infinitesimal," I say, getting kind of worked up myself.

"I have two things," says Benny. "Is radiation a kind of technology, and will you have hair?"

My having hair again has been a primary concern for Benny for months now. He climbs into our bed each morning and vigorously pats my sprouting head. "You rubby little fuzzball I'm going to rub you all up because you are the softest thing."

"Yes!" I say. "Radiation is in fact ultra-high-tech technology! And doesn't affect your hair at all!" I can hear all the exclamation marks in my voice.

A week later when Veterans Day rolls around and the kids have no school and John is off work and I have to be at Duke, I think: *perfect.* Let's all drive over to Durham and we can eat a hip foodie lunch on Ninth Street and browse through actual paper books at The Regulator and we'll take the kids to see the Duke campus and the impressive gothic hospital that is saving my life and where I—and their grandmother—have spent so many important hours. Plus: science!

My first Spidey sense that there might be some reason why teachers don't regularly take their eager elementary schoolers to tour hospital radiation facilities comes just as we step foot off the elevator into the waiting room—the same waiting room where I wait every day, where I have my usual seat and say my usual hellos and chat with the usual suspects and settle in for the usual routine.

Radiation happens in the basement—Level 00. There is a grand piano in the foyer where a med student has dropped his backpack and is playing "Wind Beneath My Wings."

Suddenly I am aware of so many wheelchairs. So many unsteady steppers. So many pale faces and thin wisps of hair and ghostly bodies slumped in chairs. Angry, papery skin. Half-healed wounds. Growths and disfigurements straight out of the Brothers Grimm. So many heads held up by hands.

These days, these are my people—the Feeling Pretty Poorlies— but I haven't really seen us as we *are* in a long time—the (mostly) walking wounded of the cancer militia. We're kind of disheveled. We're often asymmetrical. We're wearing comfortable pants and bright scarves. We tend to either smile too quickly or not at all.

I watch my kids taking it all in—seeing me among my other kind. They are not the only children in the waiting room—school is closed across the state—and I see them all scanning the room for each other with urgency, like we look for channel markers in the fog.

When I tell Marie, my radiation therapist, that Dr. Rosenblum had said it would be okay if my kids came and took a peek at the machine, I mistake her skeptical eyebrows for being inhospitable. "Sure, if that's what you want."

When we get back in the linear accelerator room, she starts

185

to explain to the kids how everything works. "Your mom lies in there," she is saying. "We keep the lights off so they don't mess with the radiation."

I notice Benny won't stand all the way inside the room and that he keeps glancing at the oversize radiation symbol on the twelve-inch-thick door. Somehow I hadn't noticed the sign or the thickness of the door before. It's like the opposite of a nuclear fallout shelter, keeping the damage within.

Marie turns on the enormous machine to show how its monster arm can rotate to both take X-rays and deliver the radiation beams. The floor opens up beneath it to accommodate its massive orbit around the radiation board, and I see Freddy's body visibly stiffen.

To be honest, I hadn't realized that all this time during my treatments the floor had been opening beneath me like some Tony Stark–designed doorway to hell, and I sort of wish I'd kept it that way.

"I'm ready to go now," says Freddy firmly. Fearless Freddy. Freddy who injects himself with his own insulin shots, Freddy who goes downstairs alone at night to get a glass of water, Freddy who marches into the bathroom when his brother spies a stink bug and dispatches it into the toilet with his bare hands, Freddy who sat for close to an hour on the corner of the bed where my mom's body lay, stroking her legs the day after she died.

"I'm done, too," said Benny.

In the hallway, we step aside as two techs angle a hospital bed around the corner. Under a mountain of white blankets, only a face showing. I cannot tell if the face is male or female, old or young. Only that the face is not well. Only tears leaking out of the closed eyes.

Neither of the kids have a single question for the techs. They usually live for the question portion of everything. Last summer when we visited Thomas Jefferson's lesser-known house, Poplar Forest, the tour guide ran late fielding questions from my kids: *Did Jefferson have a dog? Did he die of cancer? Did he like to go camping? Do people enjoy being president?* Last year, at the open house for kindergarten, Benny raised his hand in front of the entire parent-student population when the principal asked if there were any questions and said into the microphone, "Um, so what are you supposed to do if you're just really nervous about starting kindergarten?"

But here in the radiation chamber: silence.

That night at dinner my dad asks them what they thought of the trip to Duke.

"It was completely terrifying," says Freddy matter-of-factly.

"I hated it," says Benny. "I wish I hadn't seen it."

"It was pretty intimidating," John admits. "I guess I just hadn't realized."

My dad and I look at each other. "Whoops! I guess I just damaged everyone for life a little," I say.

"Yikes," says my dad. "Sounds intense."

But then the next morning: We are bumbling through our regular routine—me checking homework sheets while I drink coffee on the couch before getting myself dressed for radiation, John knotting his tie and packing lunch boxes, the kids shuffling into their shoes and coats—both boys come sit with me.

"Good luck at radiation today, Mom!" says Benny, rubbing my head. "I hope you're not scared, but if you are you can hug MacDuff when you get home."

Sometimes I think Benny conjured MacDuff from one of his recipes.

Freddy gives me a hug. "Guess what, Mom—I think I've finally figured out what I want to be when I grow up. A writer!"

19. Level 00

Chris has a painful new nodule on his kidney, and he's started looking more and more yellow. Margie's husband won't eat. The loud, nervous woman who is always on her cell phone has half her head shaved today. "Yeah, I'm downstairs on Level 00," she is saying, "you know, with the nukes." The man I sit next to when I get called back to the gowned area is so hugely tall that his gown looks like a blue napkin barely covering his naked thighs.

"You got you a nice tan going," Marie says as she readies the machine and examines my chest and my mastectomy scar. It's my twenty-seventh treatment of thirty. The skin is torched, even though it never feels like it's burning during the treatments. "Looks like that part of you has been to Hawaii."

"Aloha," I say when we're done, floating out of the nuke room in my gown, back toward the changing rooms.

"Aloha!" the techs call, the three of them clustered in the hallway in their scrubs, two of them waving slowly like my cruise ship was just pushing off, Marie looking past me, beckoning the tall man back from the gowned area.

You see the same people every day and then suddenly you stop seeing them. You never know if they finished treatment or if it was something else. We ask around after each other but no one ever knows for sure. "Sorry—HIPAA," the techs say.

*   *   *

"I'm so tired of this place," I text to Ginny one morning from Level 00. "I'm not in the mood. You know how it takes a certain amount of energy to just *be* at the cancer center? I don't have that today. I don't even feel like making eye contact with anyone."

"I would love it if you would just lose it," Ginny texts back. "Stand up on a table and tell everyone to go fuck themselves. Even the volunteer with the warm blankets and the dude playing the piano."

I scowl a little at the piano player who is playing the *Cheers* theme song when I go to fill up my water bottle. Immediately I feel better.

"How is Larry's appetite today?" I have the energy to ask Margie when I get back to my seat in the waiting room.

20. Its Very Nature

"Let us make good use of our time," writes Montaigne in his final essay. "We still have so much of it that remains idle and ill-used."

He would not approve of how I have taken to sleeping in, how I spend the evening browsing seventy-two pages of ankle boots on Zappos, how I obsess over hair styles in magazines my sprouts and I are years from achieving.

Montaigne, the aging man, on life: "I am making myself ready to lose it, without regret, but as a thing that is lost by its very nature."

Me, some nights, tucking the boys into their beds, singing an old camp song my mom used to sing: "*Mmm*, I want to linger here / *Mmm*, a little longer here / *Mmm*, a little longer here with you."

STAGE FOUR

1. Darkest Day

It is the darkest day and Christmas week. Class parties, holiday recitals, sugar cookies and gingerbread men, that uneasy word *survivor* fluttering around us like those last leaves on the oak. It has been almost a year since diagnosis—weeks since I've seen Dr. Cavanaugh—and I am on the second-to-last of thirty radiation treatments: the final step of my cancer protocol. My mom has been gone almost exactly four months.

My lower back has been bothering me since I started radiation—sometimes an ache or a throb, other times more of a spasm—but I have been going to physical therapy and trying Pilates in an attempt to rebuild my core strength, which has been decimated by months of chemo and decreased activity.

I see my radiation oncologist, Dr. Rosenblum, each week, and each week—with great sympathy in her eyes—she commiserates about the woes of back pain. She had a bulging disc when her son was a toddler. She prescribes painkillers and muscle relaxants. She sets up a referral to an orthopedist: She is concerned I have a slipped disc.

Some days I can hardly get out of bed. John brings my dinner upstairs. The kids act like they are visiting me at a nursing home. "How have you been, Mom? Can we get you anything?"

My dad brings me a heating pad and a back brace and my mother's old walker. He sits on my bed and rubs my feet.

"Oh my God, I hate that walker so much," I say. It is covered in tan Burberry fabric. But it helps me get out of bed, shuffle to the bathroom. "This is pathetic," I say over and over. Sometimes I wince and curse if my back starts to spasm while I am walking. The kids hate it. I see them freeze when I yelp.

"Can you not do that anymore, Mom?" says Freddy. "It's scaring me."

My mother broke her back three years ago—multiple myeloma attacks the bones—and she was in ungodly pain for a couple weeks. I am a little worried about the connection, but my pain improves from time to time, and my dad and John keep reminding me: *You are not your mom. It isn't helpful to compare your situation to hers.*

When the pain gets even worse, my dad shows up with the portable bedside commode my mom got after her back broke. I haven't seen it since the weeks when she was dying, before she lost the use of her legs. She was so weak that we would need to stand beside her to hold her upright—her bruised arms trying to grip ours.

"You haven't earned your place in this world until you've wiped your mother's bottom," she joked to me and Charlie.

"Oh please, Mom," I would say, "Montaigne would say you haven't *lived* until you've wiped your mother's bottom."

Later it was diapers.

"Now this is more like it," I said when she would lie there muttering *I'm sorry I'm sorry I'm sorry* as we would roll her from side to side, perfecting the art of withdrawing the used chuck at the same time as lying down a fresh one. *"Now* we're really earning our keep on this planet."

"Oh, fuck that thing," I say when my dad walks in with the portable commode. But since the moment yesterday when I tripped on the sidewalk, I have hardly been able to move. *Step on a crack, you break your mama's back* I keep repeating to myself.

I can't sleep, and when I am able to manage to even get on the toilet seat, the pain is such that I can't relax my bladder enough to pee.

"I am suffering," I say to John in the night, feeling a little melodramatic but also thinking: Yes, I believe this is what suffering is. John drives me in for treatment the next morning and I need a wheelchair.

"Don't you think I should be taking you to the ER?" John says. I can tell he's trying to hold it together.

"No! That's insane," I say. "We're already at the hospital. We're fine."

The receptionist slaps a yellow FALL RISK bracelet on my wrist. Marie and the other techs are playing *A Motown Christmas* and dancing. Someone has made bags and bags of snickerdoodles. I can't get on the radiation table without a spasm.

"This is getting ridiculous," says Marie in the kindest way someone can utter those words. "I think we need to page Dr. Rosenblum."

A bus. A cough. A rusty nail: Death sits near each one of us at every turn. Sometimes we are too aware, but mostly we push it away.

Sometimes it looks exactly like life. Orange: The colors of the sky are the same when the sun rises as when it disappears.

"Dying isn't the end of the world." What would Montaigne have made of my mom's little quip?

When Montaigne was thirty years old, his soulmate and best friend, Étienne de La Boétie, died of the plague—sudden and gruesome. Montaigne wrestled with love, horror, and a rudimentary understanding of contagion at La Boétie's bedside and then recorded his friend's death with unflinching detail in a letter he later wrote to his father. He adored La Boétie so deeply: "The greatest living [man] I have known . . . truly a complete soul whose beauty shone forth in every direction." The loss provoked much of Montaigne's signature commitment to live with an awareness of death in the room—an awareness of being always in suspicious country.

Someone pages Dr. Rosenblum. There is a stretcher. We are wheeling through corridor after corridor. I'm no longer in the radiation wing of the cancer center.

In the Emergency Department, death enters the room looking like a young, cheerful attending. "Good news is," he says, scooting close on the rolling stool, "your labs look mostly normal."

"But one thing to note." He squirms a little on the stool. "It seems from the MRI that you do have a significant fracture in your spine, at the L2 vertebra. And the way it is broken is very worrisome. It's not a trauma break. It's a pathological break, likely caused by a tumor that has metastasized from your breast."

"Okay," I say. I can't look at John. "Any chance it could be anything else?"

"I am so sorry, but no," he says. "I'm so sorry. I hate telling people these things and I'm not very good at it. We're going to admit you upstairs. You will probably have surgery right away."

A stream of doctors after that—one, a radiation resident I have come to know, crouching down to eye level with me, gripping my hand and not pushing away her tears. Then a surgeon. Then a neurologist. Then Dr. Rosenblum standing over me with the face of a mother whose daughter is very late for curfew. She keeps patting my hair: "How could this have happened? I am so, so sorry."

John's eyes from the visitor chair reflect my own face back to me again and again: *Wait, what?* We kept asking each other, *What?*

2. Helicopter

Suspicious country: ninth floor, oncology ward. Outside the window, a view of the helicopter taking off from and landing on the hospital roof. Quieter than it should be, the rotors spinning long after the frenzy of action disappears. "Your kids are gonna love that when they come visit, aren't they?" says a nurse who I can't see, who is typing on a computer somewhere behind me.

Do I know the answer to this one? Benny used to love fans and helicopters as a baby. He called helicopters "cagooies." Is that different from being thirsty? I half think through the morphine. I am extremely thirsty, and that thirst seems in this moment to be the hardest problem I've ever been asked to solve. I smile just in case that is what I am supposed to do. *Or was Freddy the fan lover? No. Definitely Benny. Freddy loved lights.* I have been admitted up here. I almost remember that. John was here. *Where are the kids? Who has the kids?* Everyone has the kids except me. *Who has the ice chips?* A doctor has just finished talking; a doctor is about to talk. It is Christmas Eve. I have had surgery. They have removed my L2 vertebra, a big lump of cancerous mush. They have installed a titanium cage with impressive screws that they show John on X-ray before I wake up, and then they email him a picture to show me.

"You are doing great," says a nurse. "They've cleared you to try standing up. Do you want to?"

I don't know the answer to this either, but then I am standing up. John is taking a picture. "Wow!" he is saying. He is putting it on Facebook. "Oh my God," says everyone I know. "Amazing!" Facebook is saying. "Can't believe this is happening to you! What can we do?" I am scrolling and scrolling. "Thank you," I am saying to Facebook. "I love you so so much. More than anything in the world. You are so beautiful."

John texts: "Maybe you should put your phone away and try to get some sleep. Maybe not the best time to be on Facebook." I look around the room. He is not here. He is nowhere. It is too dark to see what the helicopter is doing. I imagine the rotors: silent, still. Maybe no one will need them Christmas Eve. Now John is calling. Now he is a voice.

"I am in Greensboro—at your dad's. I have the kids. Charlie and Amelia are here. So is Jennie." Jennie, John's sister and one of my closest friends, lives in Tucson. Everyone has arrived for Christmas. "Jennie needs to talk to you for a minute," says John.

"I am trying to figure out stockings," she is saying.

I remember now I never wrapped the kids' presents. My back hurt too much, the paper and tape was too hard to get to. In the back of the linen closet behind the sheets, I tell her. And in the little cabinet next to my bedside. And in my closet. And above the refrigerator. And there's something in that T.J. Maxx bag behind the green chair. That deck of Harry Potter playing cards is for Freddy. The Pokémon watch is for Benny. Sugar-free gummy worms and chocolate wrapped to look like a hamburger. Jennie is laughing: "How on earth are you remembering all this?" She is also part crying: "Can't wait to see you. Will I get to see you?"

At some point in the night I wake up: John is back. I can see his outline asleep in the uncomfortable chair. "There is something I need to tell you," I say to him when he stirs. "There are tickets. Two tickets to Paris in our names in my email. For your birthday."

"What?" he says, not quite awake. "What are you talking about?"

"For the end of January," I say. "It was supposed to be a surprise."

He is turning forty in a couple weeks, and I wanted to take him to France after our tough year. It was a splurge, an impulse. We lived in Paris as newlyweds when John was in graduate school—before law school—and we haven't been back since having kids. It's his favorite place on earth: He makes sense there in a way I have never made sense anywhere.

"Seriously?" he says, trying to roll over in the chair. "You might have gone a little over the top if this is your way of letting me in on the surprise."

"I want you to know the tickets are there." I say. "Just in case."

"Okay," he says. "I can call the airline in the morning and try to cancel."

"No," I say. "We're going to Paris. I don't know how exactly, but I'm going to Paris with you."

"Okay," he says. I can hear his breathing slip into sleep again.

The Bright Hour

A few hours later—Christmas morning—I'm awake again just before dawn: the shape of the dark helicopter against the darker sky. The rotors are still. "Merry Christmas," says a nurse who is measuring my urine into a jug in the bathroom. "Do you want some pain meds? Do you want another stool softener?"

A man named Nurse Jon shows up in my hospital room while Tita and my dad are sitting with me. He tells us he moonlights as a stress management specialist when he's not working the oncology floor. He has a hypnotic voice and an almost eerie command of the room. He purrs to us about breathing techniques and mantras and allowing ourselves to be held by the bed or the chair. "You soften your belly," he says. "You send your breath there. Softest belly. Softest breath. You let your muscles relax: soft belly. You let the world hold you up."

"May I demonstrate my techniques?" he asks, but already we are under some kind of spell.

My dad has his eyes closed. Tita leans back in her chair. Time stretches and bends as he guides us with his voice into an impeccably quiet place. I feel my morphine controller fall out of my hand, but do not reach for it. Nurses and techs seemed to hover at the door, but sense his spell and are uncompelled to disturb us.

Only one person knocks at the door and it is Dr. Cavanaugh. It's the first time I've seen her since I've been at the hospital. She smiles, but in her ocean eyes I can see all the trenches and ledges of a cancer doctor.

"I don't ever come over here," she says. "Just know you're special."

Then when she sees Nurse Jon, she freezes and starts to back out. "Oh, it's you!" she says. "I'll come back later!" I cannot emphasize enough how unusual a stance this is for Dr. Cavanaugh.

"No, no—please come in!" I insist, and so she finds a space to sit on the edge of my bed, joining the four of us in my closet of a room.

She is unusually calm and relaxed in his presence—*I bet anything she has one of his breathing CDs*, I think—as he seems to disappear into the corner of the room while she talks about my latest scans: Right now the cancer is focused on the spot on my lower spine. Surgery stabilizes the spine, but can't get rid of all the cancer. We will do radiation there. This won't get rid of all the cancer either, but it should help with pain. A few spots higher up the spine are lighting up, and we will keep watching them. CT scan of the organs looks clean. Brain scan: clean. We will rescan in a couple weeks, we will make a plan.

"I'm not going to say I'm not worried," she says. "Some patients in your situation don't make it to their first set of scans. Others go for a couple years. We'll have to see."

I try to soften my belly. I try to feel for the world holding me up.

"Listen to what this man has to say," she says as she leaves, glancing at Nurse Jon in the corner. "Not to scare you, but what he has to offer you is way more valuable than anything I have."

*   *   *

Later that night Tita texts to say she got back to Greensboro safely but that Drew has just been in a car accident down the street from our house.

"He's okay," she writes. "Maybe a broken rib. He ran the red light down at the corner. Didn't have the kids in the car. Other person is fine, too. He says he was distracted and never saw the light. Car likely totaled. But he's okay—I promise. Do some Nurse Jon breathing. Get some morphine sleep."

Later, when I am home from the hospital, she tells me the story of getting the phone call and packing the kids into the car in the rain and driving the three blocks down to the corner. The sirens and the ambulance and people standing around and the cars in the wrong places in the road. "I knew he was alive because he had called me," she says. "But I couldn't figure out how to believe that he was okay, given what I was seeing."

I know just what she means. It's how I've felt every second since the doctor came to see me in the emergency room.

Much later Drew tells me he had been crying. He had run to the nearby grocery to buy eggs and pork chops after Tita returned home from seeing me. He was half-aware in the store that he was not thinking clearly.

"I really don't remember any of it," he tells me. "Only screaming in the car, after the airbag." I know Drew at Christmastime: He cries in front of the tree late at night with all the house lights off, drinking scotch and listening to Joni Mitchell's *Blue*. He cries when his sons pad down the stairs in their footie pajamas.

I know this crying is different, and that my situation is complicit. I am still waiting to cry, and to feel the slam of my steel body crashing into another.

When my family comes to the hospital on Christmas Day, everyone squeezes onto my bed for lack of a better option. *Where would my mom sit?* I am thinking. *There is no room for my mom in this new situation.*

The boys completely ignore the helicopter when I point it out, and I don't push it: Perhaps they have already outgrown these sorts of spectacles—driving around town, I pointed out John Deere tractors and earthmoving equipment for years after they stopped caring. They are dying to show me a PowerPoint presentation that Jennie has helped them make on their new laptop of the Christmas I have missed at home. *Merry Merry Merry Mom*, it says. *Wish this wasn't happening!*

As they are getting ready to leave Freddy asks me: "So, have they had to send that helicopter out today?"

"No, not today," I say.

"That's good," he says, resting his head on my shoulder.

3. Little Disc of Ruin

For years I have had a recurring dream that I am choking on a battery. Different types of batteries: triple A, 9-volt, lithium watch. Each time, I awake with panic, and I can always feel the very real sensation of the hard shape disappearing down my esophagus. *The crisis has passed,* I think, coughing and gasping for breath, *but I am still doomed.*

My first night home from the hospital, I wake up from a battery dream around 2:00 a.m. I had fallen asleep hard without brushing my teeth or washing my face or taking off my clothes.

But then suddenly: the battery, panic, then everything else — the unreturned library books on the table by the front door; the unplayed voicemails; the unwalked dogs; the uncollapsed recycling; unread emails; unwritten thank yous; unfinished parenting; the universe coming undone at the seams.

What is the hard thing you are swallowing tonight? I lie there asking myself. *Oh, just mortality. Oh just a little disc of ruin.*

Forty minutes into the freak-out, I think of Nurse Jon: soft belly, support of the world, a positive mantra embedded into the inhale and exhale of each breath. *Thank / you* I find myself saying. *Thank* and then *you.* And then the sun is brightening the sky and the kids are crawling into the bed.

Emerson's journal, 1838: "I am cheered with the moist, warm, glittering, budding and melodious hour that takes down the narrow walls of my soul and extends its pulsation and life to the very horizon. That is morning; to cease for a bright hour to be a prisoner of this sickly body, and to become as large as the World."

My cousin Bonnie arrives in Greensboro several hours before midnight on New Year's Eve. She has taken the train down from Washington, DC, where her girlfriend's father is dying of prostate cancer.

"Bonnie's Mortality Tour, 2015!" I say when we do a modified version of one of the fierce hugs we've been giving each other our whole lives. She's been living in San Francisco for the last sixteen years—working as a massage therapist and now training to be an occupational therapist, and we don't see each other very often anymore. A few days at the summer house in August, if we're lucky.

"Put me to work right now," she says, rubbing her hands together, then over my head, my neck, my back. Bonnie has always represented to me the very epitome of my family: She's strong and fearless and brilliant and magical, and her startling blue eyes look unnervingly like RWE's. She sailed around the world with her parents and brother as a kid. In one of my favorite photographs of her she is shimmying up a palm tree in her bathing suit. She rode for an all-lesbian bike messenger service in San Francisco. She has a huge scar shaped exactly like Newfoundland on her inner calf from a motorcycle accident she had as a child.

"I have brought massage oil and board games and origami

paper and spices for the most delicious Moroccan stew in the universe," she says.

Later in the evening—an assortment of family and friends downstairs playing charades and drinking and laughing, the kids running around like wild animals, John and my dad grilling New Year's Eve lamb—I'm lying on my bed while she rubs my feet.

"So, it turns out I'm kind of dying," I say to her. I haven't spoken this directly to anyone yet.

"Yeah," she says. "So, what's up with that? Why do you always have to be the first of us to do everything?"

"Can you teach me how to make origami cranes?" I say.

"I thought you would never ask," she says.

Back when I was in the emergency room, the attending had said, "I don't know what exactly will happen next, but you know that metastases put you at stage four. This is clearly an aggressive cancer. It recurred before we even finished treating it. It's probably time to put your affairs in order and make a bucket list, as hard as that is to hear."

I had been stumped by the bucket list. It depressed me: "Oh my God I am so lame I can't even come up with an interesting bucket list," I whined in the hospital.

"How about a 'fuck-it' list?" John suggested at some point. "Sort of the opposite. What can we just say 'fuck it' to and send splashing off into some sewer and not bother ourselves with anymore?"

The catch is: it turns out not many things.

I want all of it—all the things to do with living—and I want them to keep feeling messy and confusing and even sometimes boring. The carpool line and the backpacks and light that fills the room in the building where I wait while the kids take piano lessons. Dr. Cavanaugh sitting on my bedside looking me in the eyes and admitting she's scared. The sound of my extended family laughing downstairs. My chemo hair growing in suddenly in thick, wild chunks.

Light sabers cracking Christmas ornaments. A science fair project taking shape in some distant room. The drenched backyard full of runoff, and tiny, slimy, uncertain yard critters who had expected to remain buried in months of hard mud, peeking their heads out into the balmy New Year's air, asking, *Wait, what?*

4. The Perfect Couch

Were I healthy enough right now, I would be sipping a glass of complimentary wine and running my hands over an exquisite accent pillow in an impossibly hip showroom called something like Space or Lust, while a sales assistant speaks to me of the virtues of aniline versus semi-aniline leather.

"So you really think kiln-dried hardwood is worth the extra expense?" I'd be asking. And, "Does this come in a three-seater?"

Instead, I'm propped in bed on a dozen pillows with my laptop, perusing online furniture stores: West Elm, Joybird, Crate and Barrel and something called Chairish.

I am an Internet sofa-shopping fiend. I take breaks only when the oxy overwhelms me and my head starts to loll. I cannot rest until I have considered every midcentury-modern-with-a-hint-of-bohemian sofa the worldwide web has to offer. I pour over design sites like Apartment Therapy, Design Sponge and Domino: searching, searching.

Since John and I got married sixteen years ago, we have never had a real grown-up couch. We've had plenty of well-loved misfits: "as is" Ikea specials, parental handoffs, craigslist semi-miracles, roadside rescues. First we were broke, and then we had babies. It never seemed like the right time to splurge on anything nice.

And the misfits have been fine. We're not fancy, and our taste is eclectic. Our house is full of objects that are stronger on personality than looks: the wood box my father and uncles sat on as children to lace their boots for sledding, a lumpy chaise by the front window in the world's coziest reading nook.

Anyway, whenever we have needed to get down to the serious business of life, we have always preferred to retreat to our bed: our war room, cocoon, escape hatch and, at times, dining room.

But these days finding the perfect living-room couch has begun to feel like the most important thing I've ever done.

Except, just when I find one I love, it turns out I can't click "buy now." And commitment issues have not generally been my problem. Houses, cars, job-switching, kid-having, plane-ticket-buying, restaurant-choosing, shoe-shopping, mastectomy: Bring it. Usually I just pick a good-seeming option and don't look back.

Within ten minutes of meeting John in the graveyard, I had already mentally signed on for life—although I waited at least a week to tell him that.

But the couch. I can't do it. Maybe I'm holding off until after my next big oncology appointment, as though something Dr. Cavanaugh may say will help determine whether I am willing to spend the extra money for Dacron batting and polydown cushions. She promised some new thoughts about treatment options: immunotherapy, clinical trials, off-label drugs, acupuncture, the dreaded "watchful waiting."

It's a complicated calculus. On the one hand, a basic cost-benefit analysis: How much money do I want to spend on something I may not be around to really enjoy? On the other: Isn't buying an expensive couch a kind of lovely expression of hopefulness? And after I'm gone, don't I still want guests in my home to feel comfortable and stylish? Then again—O darkest demons!—maybe I should buy something hideous and uncomfortable, something the woman John remarries will be forced to keep because the dead wife bought it.

Despite all the pamphlets the social workers gave us when I was in the hospital, we don't really know how to talk to the boys yet. They know about the cancer and the back break, but they don't really know what it all means.

Instead I ask Benny, "What do you think of leather upholstery?"

"Depends if it's slippery or nuzzly," he says.

Excellent point. I think I need to take any bonded leather options—no matter how cute or economical they seem—off my favorites lists and go with top grain.

When Dr. Cavanaugh was sitting on the end of my bed that day in the hospital, I saw her glance toward the pamphlets that had been left on the bedside table: "What to Tell Your Children about Your Progressive Disease."

"Is it time to despair?" she said during a pause in our discussion about pain management and radiation, maybe reading one of the pamphlet headings. "No!" she proclaimed, staring straight at me. "No, it is not."

I trust her completely, even after the chemo failed twice and the cancer spread when she said it wouldn't. Whatever it is in oncologists that makes them want to be oncologists—that crazy mix of fierceness, optimism, arrogance and compassion—I get a contact high from it. It's like love at first sight, or touching something on fire. It's like making a choice and refusing to look back.

John is mildly new-couch averse, but he's treading carefully. He knows me well enough to understand that when I'm dissertating on the merits of tufted cushions, I'm chewing on something else.

"Custom upholstery, really? With two boys?" he asks, flipping through insurance statements on the counter. "Okay, well, I think you should get whatever you're into."

One big upside of being told I have incurable cancer is that after all these years, my husband has finally stopped smugly saying, "It's your funeral," when I make a decision he doesn't agree with.

"Did you spend thousands of dollars on the Internet today?" he asks when he gets home from work and finds me with my pillows and hot-water bottles on the not-perfect couch where he left me in the morning, a low-slung rattan situation my parents bought as patio furniture in the early '90s.

"Not today," I say.

"Nice," he says. "Do you want to go get in bed together and stare at the ceiling?"

I do. We do.

In January, the afternoon already looks like evening.

"Can you believe we found out you have incurable cancer on, literally, the darkest day of the year?" John asks as we hold hands and stare up toward the same blank spot above our bed.

"Yeah, I totally can," I say. We both laugh.

I have always loved the sound of him laughing: soft and comfortable, understated, offbeat, with unmistakably sleek midcentury lines.

He takes me gingerly in his arms as if we are awkward teenagers. My back spasms, but I wiggle closer to him until I can put my head on his chest and hear his heart beating.

Downstairs, the boys gaze at a screen on the old futon in the playroom. We will figure out what to do about them soon enough. They probably already know what's up and are waiting for us to figure out how to say it. Their very existence is the one dark piece I cannot get right within all this. I can let go of a lot of things: plans, friends, career goals, places in the world I want to see, maybe even the love of my life. But I cannot figure out how to let go of mothering them.

So maybe I don't try to figure it out. Maybe I just aim to get the couch right: strong bones, high-quality leather, something earthy and animal and real. A surface that knows something of what it was to be alive, that warms to our touch and cools in our absence.

Also: an expansive bench that fits all of us. Something that will hold us through everything that lies ahead—the loving, collapsing, and nuzzling. The dying, the grieving.

I know my thoughts have probably diverged from whatever John is thinking about in the near dark of our bedroom. He is silent. Maybe he is dozing.

Buying a sofa online, like many of life's biggest decisions, takes research and trust, but mostly trust. As I lie here—John's chest rising and falling under my cheek—I'm going to have to believe that regardless of clinical trials and future wives and free shipping, I'll know it when I find the right one.

5. Bright Spots

About the kids, my therapist says: "Okay fine, maybe they won't be okay. Maybe they'll be complete fuckups. Let's talk that out a little. Let's imagine that scenario. Give me some really good details."

"Jail," I say. "Sitting in Bojangles' by themselves on Thanksgiving trying to score heroin. Them telling John to go fuck himself over the phone and then hanging up. Them telling each other to go fuck themselves."

"That's good," smiles my therapist. "No problem going to the dark place for you."

Then he says, "But maybe they'll be more than okay. Maybe they'll be amazing. I know many people who went through loss at a young age who became extraordinary adults. Maybe they'll write award-winning movie scripts for a groundbreaking dark comedy inspired by the loss of their mother when they were children and win Oscars. Just picture them on the stage, holding that trophy."

I love this game. John is clapping loudly in the front row, a French actress on his arm. The boys clink their Oscars and point them at John. Then they toast toward heaven. "For Mom!" they say.

A retired rabbi—the friend of a friend—writes me an email out of the blue about how he lost his mother when he was nine years old. In the message, he lists all the things he remembers about his mom and all the ways she remains in his life: her favorite flower, the books she read him, her sense of humor. "She is far from a

217

hole in my life. She is an enormous presence that can never be replaced." His words are a gift that I pull out some nights and let swirl through the room, brush over my skin like a tincture.

Now that the cancer has spread, I am scanned every six to eight weeks. Sometimes I think about things I could do in six to eight weeks: gestate a baby through half a trimester, master conversational Italian, achieve rock-hard abs, binge-watch *Game of Thrones*, hike the Camino de Santiago. Instead: it's a wink, a blink, a flicker; one long exhale and a breath drawn in; John's hand running down my back, his lips brushing my neck; the length of the camp session where we met.

Tita comes with me to each new set of scans, and she knows the routine as well as I do: loose clothes; no bras, no zippers; drink lots of fluids. The receptionist loves to banter. The volunteer concierge is hard of hearing. Carla, the tech who takes patients back to the changing room, loves to talk about Jesus and the power of prayer. Sometimes she'll stop in the middle of what she is doing and sing "Amazing Grace." Tita and I aren't sure whether to sing along. We clap. "Thank you so much," I say. "That was beautiful." I hear her humming it back in the tech station. They draw blood and then inject me with radioactive dye for the bone scan, contrast dye for the CT. Tita waits in the changing room while I have my CT, but they let her come sit with me in the room while I have the bone scan. The tech operates the scanner from the adjacent control room.

For the bone scan, there is a large monitor in the room with you as you move through the machine—feet bound with an elastic band, arms wrapped in a straightjacket, warm blanket to keep you calm. Tita also gets a warm blanket, because it keeps her calm, too. The scan takes about twenty minutes, and as you emerge from the machine, the monitor lights up with your skeleton in real time, moving from the skull down the shoulders and spine and hips, and finally the legs and feet.

From where Tita sits, she has a better view of the screen than I do. We try to talk about other things: child care, her half-written novel, her root canal saga, her friend Tony's mom's upcoming surgery, the short story collection we're reading for book club, but we often end up staring at the screen. It's like watching a teacher grade your test in front of you. It's like watching live feed of the plane that you are flying in land while you're in it.

"At first I was thinking you definitely had vagina cancer but now I think it was just the radioactive stuff in your bladder," says Tita from her chair as the machine works its way along my abdomen during my most recent scan. "It's totally different from the other bright spots."

We examine the patch of concentrated light. Over the last six months—three or four scans, we have decided we are both savant bone-scan readers—clearly a second-career option. We've seen new tumors light up in my spine, my hips, my shoulder. We've predicted them all.

"Phew," I say. "Vagina cancer would be serious salt in the wound."

Tita's right: When John and I go see Dr. Cavanaugh for the results the next day, it turns out that indeed I am free of vagina cancer. More bright spots on the skeleton, though. Those, I do not seem to be able to avoid at all. Scapula, pelvis, sternum.

Bright spots, dark screen. The term "bright spot" takes on a whole new meaning, more like the opposite of silver lining: danger, bone pain, progression. More radiation. More pain medicine. More tests. Strange topsy-turvy cancer stuff: With scans, you long for a darkened screen, a blacked-out skeletal city, a subdivision of foreclosed bones. Not one lit room to be found, not one headlamp on the road, not one fireplace smoldering, not one reading lamp brightening a page of dinosaurs in an upstairs bunk bed, not one single birthday candle awaiting its wish.

No sign of life, no sign of anything about to begin.

"I heard you talking about your botched root canal," the tech said to Tita when he stepped back into the room after my last scan. "You should definitely go on antibiotics. Those things can be deadly. Hope you both have a great afternoon."

6. Vigipirate

John turns forty, and I am well enough to go to France. February—eight days. My dad keeps the boys for us, and John's mom flies in to help.

"It makes no sense that we can't go with you," moans Freddy on my bed the night before we are supposed to leave.

"It actually does make sense," I tell him as I obsess over scarves and boots. "Just not to you. Dad and I need to do this. We have a whole marriage we have to take care of. Sometimes it's important for us to focus on that."

"If you say so," says my budding tween, lumping out of the room.

I do say so, although not without my innards squeezing and aching as I also feel my world shrinking toward our cocoon of a home in the wake of the new diagnosis.

The gray-then-yellow light bouncing off the Seine in through the unshuttered windows of the beautiful apartment on the Île de la Cité that we are loaned by the grandmother of a dear friend is so exquisite that on the first night I lie awake crying until my stomach balls and aches and I spend most of the night in the bathroom.

Inside the bathroom, the room only slightly bigger than my skin, I feel safe, held up, positioned: the river pushing past on both sides of the tiny island where the first settlements dug in, in the middle of the city that has scaled and rescaled its own walls. Tucked within the building, within the apartment: the deepest interior, the bathroom at the center of the world. There: I discover a packet of unopened grief. My mother. I try to soft-belly breathe.

It is unexpected for her to find me here in Paris, but there she is. Somehow, an ocean away from my dad and the kids and almost everyone we know makes the distance away that she is feel even more boundless and profound. I want to hear her voice. She took me to this city for the first time when I was sixteen, and I remember her exclaiming about these very apartment buildings as we raced along the quai in our taxi: *Who in the world do you think lives there?! Can you even imagine!?*

In the morning when John goes out to fetch croissants and his favorite newspaper, I huddle in the chair by the front window with my phone—watching the most fortunate of Parisians wake up and scurry to work—and listen to old voicemails. "Just checking in," she says. "Wanted to hear your voice."

John and I first moved to Paris back on September 5, 2001—exactly one month after our first anniversary. We were working out the early versions of our adult selves: John was a graduate student in French philosophy in Washington, DC. I had dropped out of an MFA program at Cornell. As part of his program, John had an opportunity to teach and take classes in Paris for a year. I had a good, stable job teaching English at an all-boys' private school in Bethesda, Maryland, but one day I had stepped out of the steam of the shower in our Mount Pleasant condo, and with all the clarity of a twenty-four-year-old declared, "We have to do this." In weeks, we sold most of what we owned and I quit my job and we bought the cheapest plane tickets we could find.

Less than a week after arriving in Paris: the twin towers. That night, an ocean from home in our Ikea-filled apartment in *le troisième*, eating McDonald's hamburgers from around the corner and watching the same inconceivable dispatches from our country as the rest of the world on the tiny television set, it seemed as though John and I were all alone, drifting together into an unknown world: new language, new rules, new images to darken the dark night—one tower falling and then another.

Wait, what? we said to each other.

After September 11, Paris was quickly placed under the state of alert they call *vigipirate*—literally: vigilance for pirates—with armed police in the metro, barricades at government palaces, translucent green bags instead of trashcans on every block—and it would stay that way until we left the next summer. I ran my tongue over and around the word with my middle-school French, learned to pick it out from impenetrable French news broadcasts: *vigipirate*.

The hijackers were called *pirates de l'air*. I learned *terreur*, too, of course—and *attentat* and *état d'urgance* and *menace* and *complot*. Later: *guerre, manifestation,* ADM.

I struggled through the metro stops and grocery aisles and menus just as I struggled through the newspapers and broadcasts.

I brought my notebooks wherever I went and prowled museums and hid in offbeat cafés to write, hoping no one would speak to me. I would go whole days without saying a single world other than *bonjour* and *merci*—and still return to our apartment at the end of each day exhausted. John—whose mind gobbles new languages and cultures like I gobble soft cheese—went to class and to lectures, to movies, to parties, to bookstores and bars with French-speaking friends, to massive demonstrations near the Bastille without plotting a single escape route, to cheese stores and political rallies.

Once he begged me to come with him to an unsubtitled documentary called *La sociologie est un sport de combat* at a film house near his university—folding chairs, no heat—about the recently deceased French sociologist Pierre Bordieu. Even if the movie had been in English, I probably wouldn't have understood it—habitus and doxa, structure and agency—but I kept turning to look at John during the interminable film and seeing him literally lit up: passion and fascination transforming his face into something almost entirely unrecognizable. I was furious by the time we left the theater: cold, uncomfortable, and tears of frustration and embarrassment filling my eyes.

"I feel like you made me go to that film on purpose," I said, storming homeward down the street. "Just to make me feel bad about myself. There is no way you possibly actually enjoyed that."

I knew I was wrong even as the words came out of my mouth.

"What are you talking about?" he exclaimed, storming right beside me. "How could you not like Bordieu? He's all about art! And so charismatic and engaged! He's unlike Foucault and Derrida in that way—they're all brilliant and important, but you can't really picture them manning the barricades like you can with Bordieu."

"Please stop it," I yelled. "I don't really know what you're talking about. In my French class this week we are learning about where Loïc and Jacques bought onions!"

A few weeks after we arrived, I saw a woman trip on the Boulevard de Sébastopol outside the grocery store in our neighborhood—her heel buckling off the curb, and the contents of her handbag scattering on the crosswalk, a dangerous sound like bullets. I watched a tourist couple lurch around to the shrapnel of lipsticks, compact mirrors, peppermints—and a *gendarme* with a machine gun stop and grimace at her, wiping his forehead.

No one offered a hand to help her up, including me—although she quickly stood and smoothed herself. "I am fine," she said loudly and a little defensively, in a British accent. "Don't touch me."

I felt like that woman for most of the year we lived in Paris: stumbling, on guard, and out of place; insisting on aloneness and terrified of being alone. Some nights John and I would argue until we fell asleep midsentence. Others, we would grab dinner and then stand and kiss in the street.

"I just want you to love the same things I love," John would plead.

"I'm trying," I would say. "But I feel like a faker. Like any second someone is going to find out that what I really want to be doing is sitting on a quiet porch at sunset drinking whiskey."

"I'm a faker, too," says John, burying his face in my neck. "And I don't hate porches and whiskey. Please just fake it with me here for a little bit longer."

"Okay," I say.

I make a group of expat friends. I adopt a regular café in the Marais. I go to poetry readings and join a writing group. I take a workshop where the instructor tells me that my poem about traveling in Italy with my mom would be much improved by being cut up into little pieces and randomly reordered. I complete a manuscript of poems.

One day I find a fallen poster in the street for a showing of *La sociologie est un sport de combat.* I squirrel it away and when we are back in the United States, I have it framed and I give it to John for our anniversary. It still hangs in our living room.

"Aha!" says John when he unwraps it. "I always knew you secretly loved that film!"

Fifteen years later—when we return to France as my back is healing—Paris is back under *vigipirate* in the aftermath of the night of terrorist shootings around the city several months earlier and the attack at *Charlie Hebdo* the previous year, just days before my original diagnosis. As we snuggle on a sunny bench at Place des Vosges, I watch passersby toss ice cream cups into the green-bag trashcans. When several sirens soar by on a nearby boulevard,

I watch people pause and glance over at the nearby *gendarmerie* and a waiter at the café on the corner step into the doorway, look around. There is a chill in the air, and soon it will be time to duck in somewhere for a drink.

John seeks out one of his favorite old haunts—the bookstore near the top of Rue Mouffetard. The store is cramped and crowded and I wait outside, resting my back against an ancient urine-soaked wall and watching through the window John wander the shelves with piles of books in his arms. Suddenly, a decade and a half later, I discover I am the woman at Sébastopol all over again: *une terroriste, une pirate, une impostrice.* I hear the sob of another siren and feel it coming for me—or in my wake. Angry tears building. Paris on alert is the Paris lodged in my heart. Everywhere I look, everyone is headed somewhere—and seems to know how to get there. Even the tourists have their maps. No one else looks to be wandering in the street with a time bomb strapped to her body, thinking of saying to those she loves most: *I am sorry. I am sorry. I am sorry for what I am about to do to you.*

In the darkened room at the Cluny museum in the Latin Quarter: *La Dame à la licorne.* The lady and the unicorn. I used to come sit here again and again to examine these medieval tapestries: their rich fantasy, their smug monkeys and bunnies and beasts, the placid stare of the gilded maiden, the notorious unicorn. They ride a small blue disk of earth through the timelessness of two dimensions. As if they know what it is to ride a disk of earth: to live, to change. As if the unknown is red and covered in flowers. The unicorn stares at himself in the looking glass.

I used to imagine that in the mirror the unicorn was seeing a horse reflected back: The immortal is spying the mortal self. I loved this, and his insouciance at the realization. *It's fine: I live and I die and I live again.* But no: I can see now that the mythical horn refracts and reflects through the mirror for eternity. This crowd is only smug because they have never existed: They are only thoughts, ideas, art—private tumults floating on an ancient, woolen draft.

In that room in the Cluny museum, the viewers stand transfixed. The lady and the unicorn's expressions are cool stares we will never quite understand. We stare back because we want to know what they will never know: what to yield to and when, why we resist so briefly. We are the living, and we must keep asking what awaits—unworried, unhoping.

For our last dinner in Paris, John and I return to an old favorite: Anahi—impossibly pronounced in French—a tiny Argentinian steak house on our old street, Rue du Vertbois, run by two elderly Spanish sisters. The restaurant is quiet because we have come ridiculously early: 8:00 p.m. We sit by the window. Parisians dash by on the other side of the glass on their way home from work. Oh right: for the rest of the world it is just another weeknight.

There is no sign to reveal the name of the place anywhere, but homages to the past are everywhere: distressed subway tiles, gilded chairs, a fading Art Deco mural on the ceiling, crowds of melted candles in each windowsill. The whole evening sparkles with *kintsugi*: the Japanese art of broken pieces. Somehow, we fit in here—among the repaired wall cracks, the patched plaster, the grouted marble. Our partial selves. Our half memories. Our half-life.

"You are forty," I say to John.

"And you will be soon," he says.

In *kintsugi*, the breakage and repair are integral to the history of the object, rather than something to disguise. *Kintsugi*: the champion of the middle-aged, the ragged, the sick. I bunch my winter coat up behind me in the seat to support my back and reach for the menu in the too-dim light.

The ownership has changed, but our waiter assures us that with the exception of some small "*frenchifications*," much else is the same. Craft cocktails, it appears, have come to Paris. John drinks a "Bulleit Sour"—bourbon, egg whites, and something—possibly the bitters—imported from South America. I drink a kir: delicious, but I clearly lose.

Dinner: the menu is bigger than we remember. This was the kind of place where there were three cuts of meat described on a small hand-written card and they all came on a cutting board with a grilled ear of corn and a salad and every single one was perfect. Now there are entrées and *plats à partager* and sides. We'll muddle through somehow. We are survivors in a brave new world.

We choose guacamole and ceviche to start. They bring out

229

little spiced meatballs first, which we dip in a green chili sauce. I say: "We are having mini hamburgers before our steak!" John says: "This is what I dream of hamburgers tasting like."

The guacamole comes with crusty bread. The ceviche comes with instructions: Drink from this shot glass of sugared lime juice directly after you take a bite. We obey and are pleased. We are already forgiving the menu for growing.

When the steak comes it is almost a kilo of rib eye, cooked *sanglant*, as they say: bloody. The waiter also sets down a bowl of green salad and a skillet of golden fries and our wine. There is a small dish of *chimichurri* sauce for the meat, which, as it turns out, doesn't remotely need it. The steak is more marbled than the palace at Versailles. We are two hapless aristocrats who cannot say no. We devour everything on the table. Expect one small chunk of meat that somehow made it to medium heat.

The restaurant is filling up now. We have a tipsy dinner conversation about art and memory and pain and transcendence. We can almost taste our once-selves. We make fleeting conjecture about what Dr. Cavanaugh will tell us at the appointment on Monday, but mostly we remember old things over decaf and an impeccable caramelized *pain perdu.*

"It's Proust's madeleine," I say. "They should call it *pain retrouvé.*"

"Oh, age twenty-five," John says, half laughing. "I thought I was going to be a French scholar."

I know I am not the only one who has spent the week facing

ghosts. When we left France, John left graduate school. It had not been an easy decision for him. His graduate program felt like a dead end. He applied to other programs, but funding was scarce. In the end, we decided I would try graduate school again and he would work his way toward law school where he could maybe work with immigrants and use his other languages. A writing professor in Greensboro, North Carolina, mentioned sitting on porches with whiskey.

"Instead, life made you a great lawyer," I say. "You're basically the opposite of Proust."

"Thanks, babe. You always know what to say to make a guy feel good," he says, squeezing my hands on the table.

We walk back through the Marais toward our warm-lit rooms on the Île de la Cité. Here and there a girl laughing in the street, groups of young men huddled in the dark corners of each *rue*, women in echoing heels carrying gorgeous, cavernous totes still making their way home from the office. It is cold, so although we are tired and full and my back is aching, we pull on our hats and fall into step with their brisk pace.

After scans, on the way home from Duke in her minivan, Tita tells me about an essay she's recently read about a writer who works inside a very tiny space in her home—a linen closet—that makes her feel like she is held and safe and can open herself up to say the scary things.

I am teaching myself to say the scary things.

"It makes complete sense," Tita says. "I mean, clearly the reason my novel isn't done is because I don't have a small enough closet to write in."

She has just rented an office space, and is developing a phobia of going there. She's been obsessing over how to decorate it—paint color, desk chair, rug: all the important things that prevent us from pounding out the pages.

I think of the Paris bathroom, the MRI machine. "You just have to keep furniture shopping." I say. "Fill that place up so you can hardly move in there and the novel will coming pouring out. Maybe the more you shop, the more words you'll write."

She says that this same essay reminded her of a lit class she took in college called Studies in Evil. In the Evil class, they'd read *Beowulf* and *Richard III* and *Genesis* and explored how afraid we are as a culture of images of uncontained chaos. (One example: disembowelment. We really don't like to see uncontained bowels.) The professor had called these things Images of the Abject. We contain things and give shape to things in order to be less afraid of them.

Yes. The crafted idea does this. It's why I write. The metaphor does this. The intact body does it, too. Sometimes I worry I do this instead of allowing myself to feel things.

At the Cluny museum there was a collection of life-size stone Jesuses from the fourteenth century—on the way to the cross, on the cross, dead in Mary's arms—so human and agonized and open-faced and accepting all at once. Complicated eyes, resolved lips. But I couldn't help notice that even in the most emotionally brutal pietàs, Jesus's wounds were still depicted as the daintiest of paper cuts. No chaos.

Reveal the pain, but hide the wreckage. I can hear Montaigne hollering: break it open, look inside, feel it, write it down.

One more thing from the Cluny: down the stairs from the Jesus collection, there is a bright, limestone-walled room full of rows of giant sculpted heads—most of them ghostly white, only flecked with the occasional remaining paint chip: the once-rouge of a cheek, the once-blue of a crown. Their labels read: ca. 1220, *Les têtes des rois* and *Les têtes des anges*. The heads of kings, the heads of angels. They were taken from the original façade of Notre-Dame. And then, along a separate wall, a gallery of the bodies, lined up in rows like a choir, that I suppose the heads had once belonged to. *Les corps.*

I loved staring into their huge, vacant faces. The ones with parted lips are the most interesting—as if they've been interrupted and have been waiting patiently these eight centuries to talk again. It's the face I work on while waiting my turn to apply for disability at the social security office. Patience, calm, grace. I also imagine bashing their faces in and tasting the stone as a powder.

Tita says, "What did you think of that new bright spot up by the T12?"

"Yeah, I saw that one, too," I say. I'd noticed it glowing there on the screen like a phosphorescent jellyfish in the dark current. "Guess we'll have to wait and see."

Somehow we still never know what's next. Somehow tomorrow is always the day we're supposed to have more information. Somehow now school is canceled tomorrow and the Internet is calling for a treacherous morning across the region: wet snow, turning to ice—maybe later turning back to snow.

7. What Death Is

Whenever the weather is half-decent, my dad and his motorcycle are one—cruising up the back roads into the Virginia hills in search of a lunch spot with the best fried chicken. And, on certain warm weekends, for twenty minutes or so around town, my dad and his motorcycle and Benny are one. Freddy has no interest in the bike—he has hated the noise since he was a baby—but Benny has the bug, the *need for speed* as he and my dad like to say, giving each other five.

My broken skeleton and I stay home these days.

It's not like me to allow something so reckless as my kid on a motorcycle. Of course they wear helmets and my Dad is a paragon of safety, but this is objectively not a prudent idea—or possibly even a legal one. It's something else completely: perilous and fantastic. I think of the five-point harness booster seat in my car and wonder at the incredible contortions that logic can do. I love watching Benny's arms wrapped firm at my dad's waist.

Benny tells me his favorite part about it is that he likes to holler really loudly when they are going fast. "I scream *whooooo-eeeeeeee* up into the air and it makes me feel good!"

My dad tells me that one time, on one of their more ambitious outings—about fifteen minutes in to a smooth ride just outside town—he could feel Benny's arms start to slacken their grip. And he could feel the helmet resting on his back. Benny was falling asleep.

"Come on, Benny—stay with me!" he said, jostling his torso gently to try to wake him up without startling him.

Benny woke up.

"You can't do that again," my dad said as they waited at a red light. "It's not safe. You have to stay awake so you can hold on."

"But it sure felt good," said Benny, who was able to hold it together the rest of the way home.

I think of this feeling sometimes—and I can imagine that sort of letting go: warm, dangerous, seductive. What if this is what death is: The engine beneath you steady; those that hold you strong; the sun warm?

I think maybe it wouldn't be so bad to fall into that, to loosen the grip at the waist, let gravity and fate take over—like a thought so good you can't stop having it.

8. Intervention

"I had this dream," I tell my dad one day. "Mom was back—and she was pissed at us. Ranting and raving around in her bedroom at all the things we'd let go of or weren't keeping up with. Like plants we've let die and the dishes that are in the sink and the un-vacuumed dog bed and things like that—sort of a regular Saturday morning from when she would get on one of those tears. She was telling you all the things you needed to get at Lowe's. After trying to reason with her and not getting anywhere, I pulled you out into the hallway. 'This is untenable. We have to have some kind of intervention!' I was saying. 'We need to tell her she's a ghost and she shouldn't be here so much. Is this happening a lot?' and you said, 'Well, yeah—she's here most weekends these days, and lots of afternoons when I get home from work.' I was saying, 'Dad, we need to tell her she's dead. We have to let her know she can't keep coming here and telling us what to do.'"

My dad is laughing. "That's so weird," he says. "I had basically the same dream yesterday. That I was sitting on the patio and she was raging around pointing out all the weeds I've left to grow and all the places where the garage needs patching."

My poor mother—the legacy of a taskmaster. My dad and I click two beers together on the porch and look at the sky.

9. The Point toward Which You Were Constantly Heading

We start up book club again—about six months after my mom died. It's never really a formal discussion, but one day Anne sends out an email inviting us all to come to her house. There is a shock to the ease with which we gather our chairs a little closer, adjust our banter for five instead of six. *Where did she go?* I keep thinking.

"I couldn't imagine ever doing this without her, and yet here we are," I say to the group. We sit in a circle in Anne's living room, our plates and wine glasses propped around us on tables, our books in our hands.

We've chosen Helen Macdonald's recent memoir about her obsession with training a goshawk in the wake of her father's sudden death. The book is as dark as they come—even the cover, mostly black—like each of us holding a little tomb.

"Well, this one maybe didn't have the best timing for us," says Linda. "I could barely read any of it!" We all laugh. We can't quite remember how we selected it.

"And it's definitely not for vegetarians or the faint of heart," says Tita.

The book is full of raw meat and mouse carcasses and visceral descriptions of the instincts of a predator. I loved it.

"It's weird," I say. "For me—I can't find books dark enough right now."

The things I'm loving these days: things where everything is not okay, and that's okay—or not. Montaigne incredulous: "Did you think you would never reach the point toward which you were constantly heading?"

10. The Bridge

Ginny's cancer becomes metastatic about eight months after mine. "Do you have room in your goddamn boat?" she texts from the doctor's office. "Lung and bones. Looks like our road trip down the nipple highway just hit a dead end."

The next day she trades in her Mazda crossover for a red convertible Beetle. I visit her down in Charleston the following weekend and she takes me out for a joyride: our modified Thelma and Louise moment—although we each know that we each think about pulling a stunt like that sometimes.

"I can't sleep," she says, our two sets of chemo curls blowing in the wind as we cruise up over the bridge out to Isle of Palms. "I'm just too fucking sad to sleep."

11. Embers

April, a recent scan: All my tumors are stable for now. No new growth.

These are the appointments you don't expect as a stage four cancer patient. I didn't see this part coming: respite, good news following catastrophic news.

Instead I focus on these kinds of things: a motel on the side of I-40 near Graham, North Carolina—bereft on the shoulder of an off-ramp—called the Embers Motor Lodge. I am not confident it has seen better days, but I hope it has. And I equally hope the name never ever changes. If I someday have a psychotic break and run off to have an affair with the UPS man, look for me there first.

It's generally a quiet spot—occasionally a maid's cart on the sidewalk, a folding metal chair outside the tidy dark mouth of a guest room door, a car or two in the lot. It looks like the kind of place that rents mostly by the week or month, although it's hard to take in much detail at seventy miles per hour. But over the last year on the many trips back and forth to the cancer center at Duke, this one scooter—parked outside the second to last room—keeps catching my eye. It's there almost every time.

The scooter is screaming, *Write a novel about me*: its loyal presence outside that room, the small shell of hard luggage screwed to the back for transporting all worldly possessions, the possible DUI that precipitated it, the parade of curtain-drawn days of the last year of the owner's life in that box of a room, the job she (can she please be a she?) is trying to get it together to apply for at the Waffle House just under the overpass on Route 54. The very fact of her smoldering on the lumpy mattress each night. I feel like she and I would have some stories to tell each other about this past year: waiting to catch flame.

Ginny comes up from Charleston to get a second opinion at Duke. I've told her about the scooter, and on her way to Durham she pulls off at the exit and stops at the motel. She texts me a picture from the parking lot. There is a heart-shaped wreath dangling from the crooked numbers on the motel room door.

"The plot thickens," she writes.

We name the fictive waitress Lyla. We decide she's looking for her father—Lyle—but only has an old photograph and this heart wreath she found in her mother's closet when she died. It helps us somehow to think like this, to imagine the countless vulnerabilities and stories that fill the world.

At the good-scan appointment, Dr. Cavanaugh—just back from a weekend of silent meditation—reminds me of the necessity of staying in the present with this stuff, not trying to extrapolate to the future.

"I'm not making any promises. I have no idea what this means," she says, swiveling on her stool. "But let's just take a moment to be in the moment and acknowledge this, right now, is great news."

The Bright Hour

She shuts her eyes and assumes a vaguely meditative stance and takes some soft-belly breaths while I gaze at her.

Then, fluttering open a moment or two later: "You know—hold it not too tight and not too loose—isn't that what the Buddhists say?"

Oh my God, yes! I want to yell. And: *How?!* This is the very crux of my whole existence. And honestly, of course—all of our existences, whether we realize or acknowledge it or not.

I am reminded of an image that one of my cousins—a woman who lost her husband to a swift and brutal cancer last year—suggested to me recently over email: that living with a terminal disease is like walking on a tightrope over an insanely scary abyss. But that living without disease is also like walking on a tightrope over an insanely scary abyss, only with some fog or cloud cover obscuring the depths a bit more—sometimes the wind blowing it off a little, sometimes a nice dense cover.

Speaking of abysses, when we get home after the good-news appointment I do my first googling ever of survival rates—meaningless as I've been reminded that they are. They are indeed truly hideous for my situation. Nothing new—challenging to stare right into on the brightly lit screen, though.

After that I abandon the medical website and refocus my attention on the Embers Motor Lodge. An Internet hit on an obscure travel site offers me the only glimmer of history I could find about it: an anonymous contributor talking about his father, who as a teenager worked at the steak house once attached to the motel alongside a waitress who was married to major league pitcher Tom

Zachary, a Graham, North Carolina, native who was famous for allowing Babe Ruth's record-setting home run in 1927.

There is now a discount cigarette outlet where the Embers Steak House once was.

After an almost twenty-year career in baseball, Zachary died just down the interstate in Burlington in the late '60s. I picture his wife the waitress, season after season, simmering away as she refilled water glasses and asked diners what temperature they preferred their steaks. Let's call her Faith. I imagine her driving a scooter along Route 54.

There is a period of four days while I am in radiation treatment and traveling back and forth to the cancer center daily when the scooter is missing.

"Something terrible has happened," I keep saying to John. "I can just feel it."

"It might not always be the worst-case scenario," says John. "Sometimes it's just regular life."

I stare at him doubtfully from the passenger seat.

On one of those drives I notice the door to her room is open. There is yellow tape across the frame.

"Oh my God," I say.

"Hey, come on. It's not necessarily crime tape," John says. "It could say CAUTION—maybe they're remodeling. It could say CAREFUL WET PAINT."

The next time we drive past the Embers, the tape is gone and the white scooter is back in its spot.

We grope toward the future. Spring comes. We replant our garden. We roast Easter peeps over the fire pit in the backyard. Bunnies and mosquitos are born. Lazy curls bud and sprout from my bald head. I restart physical therapy and Pilates for my back, despite the advice from the spine surgeon that it "probably isn't worth it"— given my prognosis of a couple years.

I swallow bottles of pills and herbs and vitamins; I rub frankincense into my feet to boost immunity and lower inflammation; I practice soft-belly breathing. The kids sign up for baseball and swim team. I nurse their fevers, sign their permission slips. When he gets home from work, John carries hamper after hamper of laundry up and down the stairs.

John carries so many things.

We laugh at the dinner table. We snipe at each other. We try not to. We make summer plans. We are captivated by a news story that a hole has formed in the sun the size of fifty earths. A coronal hole, they call it—where hot plasma traveling five hundred miles per second is spilling out into interplanetary space every minute of the day.

"Are we in danger?" asks Benny, for whom the extinction of the dinosaurs is never a distant thought. "Isn't it bad that something that is burning so hot and close to us is doing things that scientists don't understand?"

"They're not sure," I say. "It's kind of a mystery. But no one seems super worried about it."

In the meantime, the articles we read tell us to watch out for beautiful side effects: the hot plasma leak has kindled a storm of dramatic auroras that can be seen from Earth. The sky is on fire, but it is basically okay.

I had a hunch my scans would be good news when we were driving to my appointment and we passed the Embers: The scooter was parked out front.

We are month to month—Lyla and me—but we are holding steady, I was thinking to myself. *A controlled burn. It's terrifying, but maybe we can go a good long way like this.*

12. What Would Natalie Portman Do?

Sometimes I'm sad about everything: the way my grilled cheese sandwich tastes, how nice my socks feel, a song John is playing in the kitchen. One time he puts on this goofy Loudon Wainwright song that was on a mix tape I used to listen to during my commute from the boys' school in Bethesda back into the District when we were newly married and everything was about to begin and it makes me burst into tears about the shortness of everything.

Freddy finds me crying on my bed up in my room — and I make no real effort to hide it.

"What's going on?" he says, climbing up next to me and patting my shoulder. "What are you so sad about?"

"The idea of dying," I say, not at all sure this is what you're supposed to say to your nine-year-old. "And how much I love you."

"Jeez. That's pretty heavy-duty stuff, Mom," he says. "When I feel that kind of sad I play my drums. You should try it sometime. I go in my room all sad and mad and when I'm done I feel like a new person."

"That's really awesome," I say, wiping my cheeks, thrilled that we have destroyed our neighbors Josie and Joe's baby's first year of sleep for a decent reason. "I should give it a whirl one of these days. I bet I'd like it."

In the movie version of my life, one day one of these waves of obliteration sweeps over me while John is at work and the kids are in school and I peek into Freddy's room and give the drums a go and sob and play and find peace. I know I'll probably never do that, but I like imagining it now whenever I look in his room. Like Natalie Portman or some other gorgeous girl whose nose doesn't swell when she cries, bent over the drum kit sobbing and raging at the universe until she can't anymore.

13. Off Battleground Avenue

Out at the science center, one of the tigers dies: Kisa, the female. I read as much as I can about it in the local paper, but there aren't many details. She was a month away from turning twelve. She had been acting strange, had a uterine infection, didn't recover from the emergency surgery they gave her. Axl, the male, has been left alone.

I can't remember the last time I've been out to visit the tigers. My kids have aged out of going to the science center as a regular activity. But reading about Kisa, I am awash in images from the survival days: strollers, diapers, Cheerios, and sippy cups. The boys running on the path past the lemurs—the forsaken lemurs— straight for the tigers. Always the tigers. *Beastie cats!* they are yelling. *I want to roar with you!*

These are the days that go on forever: Melissa and I pushing our bright strollers along the path, discussing mastitis, autism markers, Montessori versus Waldorf, vasectomy versus the pill. We are mad at our husbands who are always working, mad at our lives—so small and long. We discuss with horror the meningitis that stole our friend's daughter—sixteen months old. We cannot imagine. We cannot. We cannot. "Slow down boys!" we are calling. "You have to stay with us!" String cheeses and juice boxes and potty time and *Do you really think it is a wise choice to roar at a tiger?*

Axl prowls the perimeter. Pacing and pacing—staring down the boys and their juicy red fingers and their sticky mouths. Kisa above on the rocks—her gaze far above ours. *Nap time* we are saying now, *say bye* we are saying—and now back in the parking lot we are feeding our folding strollers into the mouths of our vans.

Who will Axl fuck now—so vigorously and so often? And who will know, so calm and certain, what threats lurk in the woods along Battleground Avenue. Who will be listening to the cars that pass, and the birds that fly overhead but never land here.

I learn from the paper that the tigers came to Greensboro from the Conservator's Center in Burlington—about a half hour off the interstate if you get off at the Embers Motor Lodge and head north.

14. Camp Radiation

It's July, and school is out—has been forever, will be forever. This morning, the dogs are at odds. They usually play fight and nip at each other's ears and paws for hours—the boys call it the Morning Match, the Afternoon Attack, and the Dinnertime Duel—but there is an edge to it today. Some yelping, a growl. One knocks the water bowl, the other slinks under the dining room table to sulk during the Morning Match. Maybe they're trying to fill the gap of the lack of conflict in the house with the boys gone.

John just left to pick them up from their week at Cancer Camp. I guess we're going to have to stop referring to it so breezily now that they'll be home. Camp Kesem. A camp for kids who have a parent dealing with or dead from cancer. A tiny beautiful loving little nest of a place. I wanted to go back up into the Shenandoahs with John to fetch them but I am not up to it. This latest radiation treatment has been grueling.

I have a new tumor on my spine—up at the T7 vertebra. Also some new cancer at the site of the L2. Plus the ones in my hips. For this treatment they give me a higher dose of radiation than what I've become used to, and because the tumor is resting right next to my spinal cord, precision is that much more important. They make me my own personal body mold to hold me in the exact same position each time.

"Scootch up in your cradle a little," says Nelson, the radiation therapist, as I lie on the metal table, "We need to line up the lasers with those crosshairs on your belly."

After forty-five minutes of angling and measuring and scootching and waiting, my arms—placed above my head—go numb and start to cramp. I'm dehydrated from spending the drive home vomiting after the last treatment. I wiggle my shoulders and Nelson's partner Kelly pops up at my head almost instantaneously. "You can't move, baby. Not even a twinge. Now we're going to have to do the imaging all over again."

"I'm so sorry," I'm saying. I'm trying not to cry.

"I know," she says, patting my thigh. "It's not your fault, but you have to try harder."

For the last five days John and I have been sitting around doing what all the other camp-sending parents do I guess: basking in our serenely quiet and clean house, eating crackers and cheese and beer for dinner on the couch while simultaneously hitting the refresh button every two minutes on the Facebook page where the Camp posts hundreds of daily photos.

"Did you see the one of Freddy photobombing the counselor photo? Typical."

"Yup. Did you see the one of Benny in the paddleboat with his stuffed animals? I think he was smiling. Do you think he was smiling?"

We've both been nervous about Benny—a profound homebody and on the very young end of the campers. And stubborn as hell.

It's Freddy we get the call about, though. Joy—whose camp

nickname is Springs—isn't Joy already a pretty solid camp nickname?—is on the line. Everyone has self-selected camp nicknames. The camp directors go by Wallaby and Lotus.

"Foxtrot and The Platypus are both fine," she says. "But we've been having some behavior problems with Foxtrot the last few days. He doesn't always listen when he's asked to do something. And yesterday during Feet on Bed, he and a friend were roughhousing and he kneed another boy in the privates."

Oh, Foxtrot.

"I am so sorry, although I am not supersurprised to hear this," I say. "Foxtrot has these issues at home as well."

"No biggie," she says, "He's a trip—smart, hilarious, super-responsible with his diabetes care. Just didn't want you in the dark on this because he won't be welcome back to Camp Kesem if this behavior continues. It's too sensitive of an environment."

"Of course," I say. I'm holding the phone lying in bed with a scented sleep mask over my eyes to keep the nausea at bay. "I get it."

Looking up helps—with nausea and when your kid is on the verge of getting kicked out of Cancer Camp.

On the way home in the car while I was puking over and over again into the McDonald's bag, my dad—my poor dad!—spotted some kind of dirigible up in the clouds over Graham, not far from the Embers exit.

"Look at that," he said—and we did, admiring its noiseless, almost imperceptible movement from where we were on the highway below. I like direction that looks aimless but isn't. Just subtle.

Just making its way without hope, without despair. Isn't that what Isak Dinesen said about writing? Same with living.

"That Platypus though," says Springs before we get off the phone. "He's his own man, isn't he. He's doing just fine." Surprises.

The long game remains a little hazy. Other than radiation, there aren't a lot of other treatment options available, although this landscape is always changing. The big hot thing in breast cancer (and many cancers) right now is immunotherapy, but it is still largely only available through clinical trials (unless, as Dr. Cavanaugh suggested, I wanted to donate a building to Duke Hospital or something).

I am not eligible for any of the trials yet, unfortunately, because I have to fail a round of postmetastasis chemotherapy in order to qualify. That's fine, but the problem is that Dr. Cavanaugh feels strongly that it is my immune system that is keeping the cancer from taking off like wildfire right now, and more chemo that is unlikely to do anything will only deplete my immune system.

"Couldn't you just pretend to take the chemo pills—if it's just to make you eligible for the trial? How would they ever know?" asks my dad.

I'm thrilled at the idea of this small act of rebellion.

Even still: All of the US-based immunotherapy trials are still currently randomized and blind, which means you only have a one-out-of-three chance of getting the actual drug and not the placebo.

The shorter game: The dogs still haven't quite settled down. John should be home with the boys sometime midafternoon. MacDuff is on alert at the front door—barking at every Saturday morning lawnmower that growls on, every weed whacker, every bike wheel that tick-ticks by.

Ellie is lying at the foot of the bed. She can no longer hear or see very well. But if she feels me roll over in the bed she's up standing at attention in a split second, staring at me. "What are we doing," she implores. "What's next?"

"I have no idea, you crazy girl," I tell her, patting her head. "Let's wait and see."

15. The List

John is a superstar dad, but now I keep a running list on my phone of the things I'm worried no one will teach my kids: table manners, how to play Scrabble without getting in a fight, long division, how to pack light, how to find the orange juice in the refrigerator.

"Let's say aloud all the people who could help Dad take care of us," says Freddy one night when I am tucking them both into the bottom of their bunk bed.

They still prefer to sleep together.

We make a list.

"Man, that's more than I can fit on both hands," says Benny with an enormous grin on his face.

Freddy reaches toward me for a hug and says nothing.

16. Jump Around

I pick up John during his lunch hour so we can go on a date to the medical supply store to buy me a cane. With the tumors in my hips and pelvis, I'm having a harder time getting around. John tries to talk me into one that is camouflaged for duck hunting and another that is clearly from some Lord of the Rings fantasy he had back in middle school, but I choose a dark blue one with a comfy rubber grip and a floral pattern that looks like bathroom wallpaper from the 1960s. I'm pretending that I'm starting a hip new craze that people don't even know about yet—like vaping or lumberjack beards or bone broth. Canes: the new frontier in walking. Like walking only better. Extra virgin, cold-pressed walking.

Two days after I get the cane, John, Tita, Drew, and I go see Grandmaster Flash in a concert that starts after 9:00 p.m. and is held in a huge parking lot downtown. We are neither the oldest nor the youngest by far. Flash himself is two years shy of sixty. We dance and get bumped around by the crowd for an hour and a half. I use the cane for an extra boost off the ground when he mixes in "Jump Around."

The next day I can't get out of bed and I have to double my fentanyl. I resign myself to the bigger-size patch. Once I go up in the fentanyl dose, it seems I never go down.

17. The Hit Woman

One night I have a dream I am being stalked by a hit man—or a hit woman, rather. She has a badge and is dressed like a lawyer, although slightly disheveled and with a French accent. She has been following me for days when I finally turn around and confront her.

"Look. You don't have to do this. It's not etched in stone," I say.

"I'm sorry," she says, holding her gun inside her suit jacket. "I do. It's my job."

"Please," I keep saying to her. "I have kids. They are little. And they need me. Can you give me just a few more years? I promise to go nicely if you can let me have a few extra years with them."

In the dream, I cry in a way I have never cried before. I am hysterical. The situation is too cruel. This is the saddest thing I have ever imagined.

"We will see," she says, shrugging and walking away. "I will see what I can do."

I tell John about the dream when we wake up.

"Oh my God," he deadpans, pulling me close, hugging me. "Imagine if something like that were actually happening to you."

I punch his arm. All day I am haunted by what I am unable to feel.

18. *Adult Supervision*

Would you believe me if I told you that around the same time that Ginny's cancer spread, a second scooter started showing up at the Embers Motor Lodge, sharing a space in the empty parking lot with the first one? A couple times they've both been gone at once, but usually at least one of them is there. One has a cover; the other is left exposed to the elements.

Ginny's lung metastases make her eligible for immunotherapy because the tumors can be biopsied and measured more precisely than mine. She's been looking for a clinical trial, and it seems there is a really good option at UNC. But even after signing a thousand consent forms and having painful bronchoscopies and long days of lab work, there is still an epic waiting period to find out if you qualify. They have to send part of Ginny's tumor to Europe. And apparently some European bureaucrat has been holding things up—or at least that's what the trial coordinator at UNC says.

The days pass—a couple weeks. In cancer time, that feels like years, decades—like the remaining days of your life are soaring by on a busy interstate.

"Still no word on the trial of course," Ginny texts one night. "I did two shots of vodka and then got into bed."

"What matters is that you're taking care of the important things," I text back. It's not yet 8:00 p.m. and I'm in bed myself.

She tells me she's started thinking about taping lectures to her

259

kids as future teenagers that her sister could email to them when the time is appropriate.

To her son, who is the same age as Freddy: "Keep it in your pants unless you are alone in the privacy of your own room or your own shower, and *do not* make your aunt clean up stiff/crunchy socks from around your room. It is perfectly fine to jerk off. Just be polite about it."

She assures me I can borrow that one if I want.

To her eleven-year-old daughter: "If a guy *ever* grabs the back of your head and tries to pull/put your face in his crotch, that is a deal breaker. (Unless he has just gone down on you . . . and even then I think it is probably time to leave.)."

I say a silent hallelujah. I have always wanted a girl, and I've always been jealous of moms with daughters. But the idea of parenting a teenage daughter from the grave sounds worse than terminal cancer.

Ginny texts me another one: "Kids: if you ever get freaked when you are making out with someone and you suddenly think *oh shit my mom can see this*, please know that *if* heaven exists, and *if* I am there, and *if* I can watch what you are doing, I will politely draw the curtains and give you your privacy. At least, I think that's what I'll try to do. No, maybe I will watch to make sure you don't do something disgusting."

I love that one; oddly, it's something I've thought about in terms of my own mom since she died, as though dying makes us more powerful parents than the living version of ourselves. Does she somehow magically now know how seldom I clean the downstairs shower? How bad I am at balancing my checkbook? That I've worn this pair of jeans three days in a row?

When our kids were littler, John and I convinced them that the word *supervision* meant a superhero-like all-seeing power possessed by some people — particularly grown-ups: *Adult Supervision, Parental Supervision*. And that we had it. For example, a sign on a hot tub that read Parental Supervision Required indicated that your parent must possess Supervision in order for you to go in that hot tub, so that they would know how you were behaving, whether they were watching you or not.

A run of good luck and intuitive guesses on our part have kept the ruse half-alive, but maybe when I die it will be strengthened just in time for tweenhood. I don't want to make them paranoid, but I don't mind fibbing to keep them honest. It's not anywhere as diabolical as the stunt that Ginny's friend Lee and her husband pulled with their kids by telling them that when the ice cream truck's music is playing that means the truck is out of ice cream.

"What if we keep our email accounts open and give your sister and John our passwords?" I reply. "That way they can get a direct 'mother is watching' email whenever necessary."

"Perfect," says Ginny. "We can have them all ready to go and my sister and John can just press send: 'Freddy, it has come to my attention that you have been looking at porn on the laptop. Not cool. Not cool at all. Disrespectful to women, and it can cause blindness. Please use your time more wisely. Love you, Mom.'"

Finally Ginny gets the go-ahead for the clinical trial. As long as she doesn't get too sick in the meantime and as long as she's not in the placebo group, she now has a one in five chance of the immunotherapy working its magic.

Twenty percent. Ginny's oncologist tells her that when it works it's a miracle, but when it doesn't it's a total dud.

"At least there's no stress at all there," Ginny says. "No giant pressure to wake up under each day."

The day before one of Ginny's lung biopsies for the clinical trial, we meet up at a fancy hotel in town for the night. Ginny brings her best friend Lee with her, and I bring Tita, and we all four sit on the patio in the fall evening, drinking cocktails at the hotel's restaurant—just like ladies out on the town. The waiter comes over and lights the gas fire pit.

"Good to see you girls out early having fun," he says. "Nice night for it."

We are, in fact, out early—since Ginny can't have anything to eat or drink after midnight. At one point in the evening, she leans toward me from her luxurious oversize patio lounger, and I lean toward her from mine and she says: "Is it fucked up that I keep buying clothes for the kids for when they're much older? Yesterday I went to the Gap outlet near the cancer center and spent a fortune on twelves and fourteens in boys' pants. And I've been browsing prom dresses."

"Totally fucked up," I say.

Meaning: My friend, that's one of the sanest things I've ever heard. Meaning: I never stop being amazed by how simultaneously cruel and beautiful this world can be.

19. Lyla

One afternoon on the way home from Duke, I catch a glimpse of someone who can only be Lyla in the parking lot of the Embers. The two scooters are in place and the door to the room is open and she's wearing too-tight jeans and holding a cigarette, talking to someone in a beat-up sports car. She's much fleshier than I imagined, bright peach skin and blond hair stringing down her back.

"It's Lyla!" I'm yelling, and John's yelling, "Jesus, stop yelling! You're going to make me crash!" and I'm yelling, "Lyla! Put down that cigarette!" and then John is saying, "Of course Lyla smokes, what are you even talking about?" and I'm saying, "I really don't like the looks of the guy in that car she was talking to."

"Well we should probably stop and go back and you should tell her that right now, along with your smoking PSA," says John. He usually rubs the back of my neck on the drive home from Duke, but now he's stopped because I startled him. I'm wishing he would start again.

Lyla can't stop making bad decisions. She spends a quarter of her paycheck on a pair of knee-high boots at the outlet mall. She oversleeps and misses her screening appointment for the Certified Nurse Aide program she's trying to get into. She's nicest to all the wrong customers at the Waffle House: the guy who is trying to make his way toward the casinos in Cherokee, the guy who suggests how she might look if she was only wearing her boots, the guy who has nowhere to stay and lost all custody of his daughter because some three-year-old kid at his mama's daycare in the apartments where they've been living spilled juice on his Xbox controller and he told the little fucker to suck his dick and now there are child sexual assault charges pending.

She does make one or two good decisions: Sometimes at night when the a/c unit conks out and the guy with the custody situation is snoring and farting and the room gets so hot her thighs stick together, she climbs onto the scooter and rides south on Route 54, out into the county, where she takes off her helmet and wastes a couple bucks of gas at top speed—which isn't very fast but enough to unstick her hair from her neck, to feel a breeze where there is none.

Other times she slips out the motel door and pads over to the back of the cigarette outlet where they leave out a couple chairs for employee smoke breaks. There, she likes to pull one chair in front of the other and put her feet up and sit and watch the interstate stretching west toward Greensboro, then Winston, and then somewhere past all the lights: the mountains, where Cherokee is. Lyle used to talk about the mountains during his truck-driving days: hundreds of miles of monsters on the horizon, darker than the darkness of the sky at night.

At the Embers, it's never really dark—with the interstate and the fast food signs and the gas station lights of nearby Graham glowing orange—like something almost on fire, like a cigarette, like something hot in her chest that says: There is no future. There is only this. The firmness of this chair holding you up. A little girl somewhere in town who doesn't understand the word *custody* and misses her asshole dad. Not Lyle, but the possibility of Lyle. This nonstop river of cars headed who knows where. Somewhere— maybe thirty miles west—a woman who cannot sleep. A woman who is dying. A woman who can't figure out how she is supposed to let go.

20. The Anniversary

A year after my mom's death—August—I've just had a round of radiation for some new cancer in my spine—and now we're on the Cape, back at the flagpole: Gin for Jan, I'm calling it, a circle of Adirondack chairs on the bluff. She loved the cocktail hour. Some of my closest friends are with us—Tita and Drew, Adam and Melissa—but otherwise it is just our new little family unit: me and John, our kids, my dad, Charlie and Amelia.

Anniversaries make me nervous—the way you are supposed to be able to summon your feelings about someone or something because they match up with a day of the year. Sometimes being in the exact place helps, because it summons the intangibles of smells and the way the light looks.

Following that logic, we should all be gathered tight in her stale bedroom—but being here on the island evokes plenty. Not only her death—do her ashes still somehow surround us in the grasses?—but her life. We are all slightly sunburned from a day at the beach, we've been taking turns in the outdoor shower, we are sipping wine from mismatched cups, the pack of kids—six boys—are running wild by the boulders, concocting a play they want to put on for the grown-ups tonight: *Revoloosh On!*, a sort of improvised *Hamilton* off-shoot featuring mostly dramatic battle scenes. We have promised to trek down to their roughshod amphitheater out by the compost pile to be their audience as soon as we've made it through the first round of drinks.

"Have you been able to feel her at all?" I ask Charlie.

"I guess if feeling the absence of her is feeling her, I feel her," he says. "I keep having the sense that we're waiting for one more person to sit down to dinner, to enter the room. Like she's in the bathroom and she'll be back in a sec."

"Yeah, I'm having that exact feeling a lot, too," I say. "And the feeling that I'm getting away with something that she is about to call me out on."

Family vacations were often the time where she most liked to keep it real. You'd be relaxing in the hot tub together and all of a sudden she'd start saying, "You know what I've been meaning to talk to you about?" and in an instant you are whirling through a universe where is it obvious to everyone but you that you have been failing at life in some deeply subtle but disturbing way, where wearing socks with holes in them is fundamentally disrespectful, where you have irrevocably spoiled your children by allowing them to negotiate for dessert after they have clearly violated dinnertime rules.

I can tell my dad has been feeling it, too: Should we go off on a picnic, even though we're getting a late start? Can we spend the whole day reading by the window? Did anyone sweep the kitchen today? No one is here to tell us what we should be doing. I keep decluttering the coffee table in the living room from a place of fear.

"I can give you a thorough talking-to, if it would make you feel better," Charlie jokes.

Usually my parents slept in my dad's parents' old bedroom, but this year he chooses to sleep in the bedroom that was his grand-mother's. So John and I take my grandparents' quarters—a big west-facing room with a private bathroom, a view of the bay, a nice draft when the predominant wind blows, and a screen door leading out onto the porch.

I sit on the edge of the bed and examine through the faded mirror on the dresser the mass of curls on my head, livelier than usual in the salt air. My face is tan; I'm wearing a tank top. I don't look sick.

"I'm definitely going to die in the winter," my mom told me once, a few years ago. "Summer is so kind. Winter always seems like it has it in for me."

Now I can feel her sitting right here on the bed with a book, late in the afternoon like this when the light shifts and the breeze picks up, my dad headed down the path for some predinner fishing just offshore in the boat. She is everything but absent. As a little girl— and even a teenager—I loved to come and find her here, to have her to myself, even though I knew it risked being told about all my latest shortcomings. Just to sit with her and enjoy the quietness around her—the way so many children seem to love to do with their mothers without understanding how we disturb that quietness with our very presence. Just now, I hear Benny galumphing down the hall toward me: "Mom! Where are you? I need to nuzzle you!"

The visceral anniversary of her death doesn't come until after sum-mer has officially passed, and of course it comes as a surprise. The

269

end of September. We are home from the Cape. The kids have returned to school. Charlie and Amelia have just arrived in town. They've decided to escape the Western Mass winter and come live down here for a little while at my dad's house while Charlie works on finishing his dissertation.

They have a new dog—Luna—a young, bouncy pit mix that likes to get in the middle of everything. She hardly ever stops moving, and she's still recovering from a run-in over the summer in the woods with a skunk. Charlie and Amelia can barely control her.

The second night after they move into town, Luna and my Dad's geriatric fat beagle Clyde get into a nasty fight over some food, and Luna rips Clyde's face up pretty badly: chunks of flesh torn from his snout. Clyde, already well on his way to complete dementia, becomes completely incontinent. The house is a minefield of puddles and piles of shit, and Clyde is too fragile to undergo what it would take to patch his face. The next morning, my dad decides to put him down. The vet offers to come out to the house.

My dad calls me: "We're doing it in about ten minutes."

"Okay," I say, jumping in the car, texting John a jumble of autocorrect nonsense at the stop sign. "Luna a Soul Train Clyde; running to my dad's; herbed late; patting him down; FUCK. None of that. We have to put Clyde down. Long story. XO."

Already the first signs of déjà vu are setting in.

When I get to the house, I can tell Charlie is kind of a mess, and Amelia seems freaked: They've had Luna shut upstairs all morning, and Clyde is wandering around listlessly in the garden.

"This is so awful," says Amelia, sitting at the patio table with her knees wrapped up under her chin.

Charlie wipes his nose.

"It's kind of fishy," I try to joke. "Every time you guys come to town, someone dies or almost dies." We all look at each other, but no one is moved to laugh. My dad and the vet show up.

The way the vet hugs and greets me, I can tell right away she thinks I'm my mother. We look alike if you don't know us very well, and I'm sure my cane isn't giving me a youthful air.

"Oh, poor Clyde!" she gushes. "I'm so sorry today is the day! He has lived such a great long life with you all."

"Thank you for being here," I say. My dad is being characteristically quiet. We're all standing around looking guiltily at our feet. I keep kneeling down and petting Clyde compulsively—more than I normally would—because I can tell my dad is totally checked out and I feel like someone should.

"Are we going to do it out here on the patio? It's such a nice day!" says the vet, "Do you want to bring his doggy bed out here? He might like that."

"That's a really great idea," I say, and my dad runs inside to grab the urine-steeped cushion, the deathbed.

We don't plan it this way, but at precisely noon—the bells on the campus church tolling—the vet injects Clyde, who lies on his bed as we awkwardly circle around him, with a very hefty dose of pentobarbital into his veins. After a minute or so passes, she checks his pulse, decides to give him another shot, and then he is gone.

The vet, of course, does not know that the color of the scrubs shirt she wears and her haircut and her general vibe remind us all overwhelmingly of Patty, my mom's hospice nurse. She doesn't know how we gathered here out on the patio the morning after my mom died—these very chairs—and felt the first day without her creep into being, how the sun felt so similarly crushing and yet warming. She doesn't know of our loss at all. In fact: She thinks my mom is me.

"You'll find grief is very strange," she says as Clyde's paws and jowls stop twitching. She is unmarried, has just lost her fifteen-year-old dachshund this year. "You think you have a handle on it, and then you don't at all."

When she hugs me goodbye, she squeezes my arm. "I'm glad to see you're doing well. I heard you were very sick. God is good."

After she leaves, Amelia and I sit on the patio. My dad and Charlie dig a big hole in the yard on the other side of the garage by the fence where Clyde loved to lie in the forsythia. We watch them heave Clyde's body from the dog bed into the earth, and then fill the hole back up.

"Won't Luna want to dig him up?" I say to Amelia.

"Probably," says Amelia darkly.

But my dad is on it—covering the wound of dirt with some junk from the garage: some pieces of plywood and a ladder.

"That should do it," he says, never exactly one for aesthetics.

"Rest in peace, old dog," I say, hugging my dad.

I have never been able to say that phrase about my mom. It

feels morbid and clichéd. It's etched on a Styrofoam gravestone that the boys love to stake into the front yard every Halloween. But of course, it's what I wish most for her, for myself: Rest in peace, Mom.

"Rest in peace," my dad says, climbing into his beat-up van to head back to work.

21. Item 18-B

John and I go talk to a financial planner because that seems like something grown-ups do. John is forty now. I'm supposed to turn forty in the spring.

The planner is nice—approximately our age, friendly, kids, knows lots of the same people we know. Seems a good match. John has told him about my diagnosis ahead of time, over the phone.

"Real sorry to hear about your situation," he says when we come into his office, looking me in the eye, shaking my hand heartily. "Can't imagine doing what you do every day."

A snarky part of me thinks, *Well, likewise*—but I'm immediately grateful for this kind man and his clarity and his handshake and his ability to do long multiplication in his head and his bright office full of stacks of spreadsheets carefully plotting out the future. He has a huge view that looks northwest, out toward the greenest part of Greensboro.

"So tell me what your priorities are," he says to us when we get settled. "What means the most to you? What do you want your life to look like?"

This is obviously a loaded question, but I like thinking about it. Financial planning, it turns out, is a fundamentally optimistic endeavor.

John and I look kind of sheepishly back and forth at each other, and then I say, "I guess I'd like to travel for as long as I can—make some memories with the kids."

"Yup," John agrees. "And I'd also really like to pee further away from the children. Like nowhere near them." He is referring to our mutual wish for a master bathroom someday.

"Oh yeah—and for them to go to college!" I add.

"Gotcha gotcha," says the planner, smiling. "All sounds good, doable." We've brought him all the important papers of our life—bank statements, tax returns, pension reports, etc.—which at home we still keep all stuffed in one giant file marked Important Papers in my twenty-three-year-old handwriting—and which he now has duplicated in a neat stack in front of him.

"So what happens next is we'll take a look at all this, run some numbers on our end, and then let you know what we think a good plan is next time we meet."

I have to miss the next meeting because of a doctor's appointment, but John hands me the impressive twenty-seven-page report when I get home: chart after chart, scenario after scenario.

"Item 18-B is kind of a doozy," he says.

Item 18-B is a breakdown of both of our yearly income and expenses by age. John's column goes up through age ninety-three. Mine stops at age forty-four.

"Yikes," I say. "He doesn't have much faith in me, does he?" My first thought is wondering if he somehow spoke with Dr. Cavanaugh and now knows something I don't.

22. Faith

A few weeks ago, Carla—the tech who escorts me back for CT scans—taped a small square of paper onto my cane where it bends into the handle. It says FAITH, all caps.

"Believe me," Carla said when she stuck it on there. "You gotta have it, and you're gonna need it."

I wasn't sure what to think. *Faith* is a word I have struggled with—a cipher I can't solve or release. I developed a habit of rubbing my left index finger over the taped tab. Sometimes out of embarrassment, self-consciousness: for wearing this word so ostentatiously displayed—as if it had anything to do with me. Sometimes more meditatively: a reminder to work harder to figure out what it's all about, a reminder to feel more at ease with the unknown, the poorly understood.

For me, faith involves staring into the abyss, seeing that it is dark and full of the unknown—and being okay with that. And if I can achieve that—BREATHE. STOP BREATHING. BREATHE—even for a quick moment, that is truly something.

Given the name tag, now the kids call my cane Faith. It suits her: her floral print, her sturdy rubber nub. "Don't forget Faith!" Freddy says with a grin. "Did you lose Faith again?" I'm beginning to think Carla was playing a bit of a prank. Some days I don't need Faith, my crutch, at all—and others I depend on her heavily. I live on fentanyl, oxycodone, ibuprofen—but Faith is what keeps me moving forward.

*   *   *

It's hard to say exactly how the pain shapes my days; it is as variable as the weather, as tomatoes, as a child. Sometimes it finds me with the first turn in bed; sometimes only after too long at a party; sometimes it is all that I am—my truest self—and other times I only recognize it on the faces and stoops of others enough to say its name. *Pain*—you are a cipher as well.

I go to lunch with friends, propping Faith on the back of the chair where she dangles and rests. My friends ask a new kind of question: *How is* today? *I hope the pain is manageable* today.

Montaigne talks about how the Egyptians at their feasts liked to present their guests with an image of death—a skeleton, a skull maybe—and a subtle entertainer who yelled out: "Drink and be merry, for such shalt thou be when thou art dead!"

Faith is my skeleton at the feast, I think sometimes. I see the young mother's double take, the kids who stare, the waiter's nervous glance, my friends who jump to adjust my chair. Maybe the skeleton at the feast is me.

23. The Reaper

For Halloween, Freddy is a perfect Slash from Guns N' Roses —
top hat, leather jacket, black wig of curls, electric guitar, rock-star
attitude. Benny is a last-minute Grim Reaper.

"What happened to being a nuzzly little fox?" I say to him when
he appears downstairs in a hooded black cloak from Freddy's Harry
Potter getup last year and a convincing scythe made of duct-taped
sticks. "I loved your little orange tail and your little orange ears!"

"Sorry," he says very seriously. "I just wasn't in the mood for my
fox anymore. I promise I'll be a fox next year. This year it turned
out I just really wanted to be a reaper."

"That's fine," I say. "I know how it goes. One minute you are a
happy little woodland critter, and the next you're death incarnate."

"Yup, Mom," says Benny, swinging his scythe over his shoulder
as he admires himself in the dining room mirror. "That's precisely
how it goes."

24. Heavy Debris

I get into a clinical trial just after Thanksgiving. Dr. Cavanaugh finds that my original tumor tests positive—at least marginally—for the hormone androgen, meaning that if we use a medication that blocks androgen in the body, there is a chance it might slow down the growth of my tumors. She is running a trial that is studying this theory.

Qualifying for a clinical trial produces some ecstatic feelings not unlike what I imagine qualifying for an Olympic trial feels like: You did it! Congratulations! All your fortitude has paid off! Gold medal in lab draws. Gold medal in initials at the bottom of the page. Gold medal in patience. It's a very odd balance: You're sick enough to get in, not sick enough to be disqualified, and you possess some special trait worth studying.

"Let's call in the trial protocol team and get you consented right away," Dr. Cavanaugh says, clearly energized by being back on a worn path, reentering a known world. *Now we're cooking with gas. Now we got us a plan, Stan.* It takes a while for it to settle in that the worn path in this instance is the path of scientific experimentation—hypotheses, data collection, waiting for the unknown.

The protocol team who runs the study takes me through dozens of pages: likely side effects, possible side effects, rare and serious side effects. There are privacy concerns, research methods. There is: You must understand that we don't totally understand.

Possible: fatigue, pain, tremors, confusion, nausea, sweating, birth defects.

There are land mines everywhere:

"We need you to have a second form of birth control in use," says the protocol nurse. I snort, thinking of our chaste evenings lately: me drooling on John's shoulder while we watch a show on Netflix about British detectives or superheroes or elite special forces units and he tries not to jostle me and prompt the need for another pain pill. I think we're all set.

"IUD? Vasectomy?" she asks.

Everyone looks over at John in the corner.

"It's fine with me!" he exclaims, putting up his hands in the air. "I've been ready for years!"

"No," I say firmly. "I'll get an IUD as soon as possible. I'm sure I can get in with my gynecologist this week."

The protocol nurse marks it down. "Okay—whatever you all decide, just let us know."

"It will be an IUD," I repeat.

"What's your deal?" John says to me when the team empties the exam room. "Why are you so emphatic about the IUD?"

"You're not getting a vasectomy. It doesn't feel right," I say, stuffing the ream of paperwork into my bag, not looking at him. "You have no idea what you might want—after."

"Jesus, Nina," says John. He hands me my cane. "I do know that the last thing I'll want is more kids. I hardly even wanted kids with you!"

"You never know what your new wife might want."

"Screw that casserole bitch," says John.

IUD. IED. I don't know a thing about land mines, except that once you step on one you can't unstep without it blowing up. Or without some special forces soldier coming in and miraculously shifting the weight seamlessly from your foot to something else — like to another person or some heavy nearby debris.

We stand like two people in the middle of that act in the exam room for some time: John's arms around me, my head in his chest, neither one of us ready to shift the weight, let go.

25. XXX

I call Ginny to tell her I made it into the trial.

"Yay!" she wheezes. "We are now both official guinea pigs of the medical system."

The tumors in Ginny's lungs have grown enough to cause her chest to fill with fluid—pleural effusion—which makes it hard for her to talk or breathe deeply. Or maybe it's the immunotherapy flare. Either way, they put in a drain to make her breathing easier.

"I basically have a tap in my back now," she says. "I'm never having sex again."

"Oh come on," I say. "I bet there is a whole subculture for people who are into that. Medical equipment fetishes. You just need to search the Internet and find them."

"Do you really think I haven't done that already?" she says— laughing, coughing.

26. The Fireplace

In his biography *Emerson: The Mind on Fire,* Robert Richardson writes that before Emerson climbed the stairs to his bed for the last time at his home in Concord—six days before he died—he insisted on closing up his study himself: fastening the windows, latching the shutters, and separating the coals still glowing in the fireplace. I picture his long body—addled by dementia, weak and feverish with pneumonia—gripping the poke, edging the ashes, nosing at the deep orange embers. Maybe they seemed beautiful— their rich, mysterious warmth.

Throughout his life, he wrote about how he loved the image of smaller flames merging into a larger fire: a metaphor for the creative urge as a conduit for spiritual connection. "A spark of fire is infinitely deep, but a mass of fire reaching from earth upward into heaven, this is the sign of the robust, united, burning, radiant soul," he wrote in his journal (1842).

The spotless orange sunrise on the hills by Walden Pond. Lyla bathed in light on the folding chair as the sun dips below the highway. My father with his hand on my mother's forehead as she rants for orange through the night.

27. Well of Mercy

I decide I need some time to write and be alone, so I sign up to spend a few days at a retreat center and convent about an hour from home — Well of Mercy. It's run by Catholic nuns, but they say they'll take anyone — in fact, my mom went there once several years back.

"It's such a gift to step away from the world for a bit," I remember her saying, "although it was really nice to come home."

The place is calm and cheerful, with huge unpaned windows staring into the woods. There are walking trails and a labyrinth and a hot tub. There are warm simple meals and warm simple rooms. Signs everywhere asking for quiet. And still, from the moment I step inside I am filled with darkness — with complete terror.

I suppose I felt it building before I even left home, as I was packing my bag in my bright, quiet bedroom that morning after the kids left for school — readying myself to leave them. I am practicing, I thought. This is just practice.

And building more as I drove along the bright, quiet highway toward the mountains — then down the country road with its goats and donkeys and lifeless tractors and leafless trees, then up the long dirt drive and down into the hollow where the convent was hidden. And building in the soft, warm bosoms of the sunny nuns who welcomed me at the door. Building in such a way that I could barely look them in the eye. Building as I closed the door to my room and set down my bag on the bed.

I've had panic attacks before, but not in more than a decade: before kids, before the diagnosis. It's suffocating: darkness looking at darkness. Like lying in a wooden box or a metal tube. Nowhere to look that is looking away. *Turning our heads ceaselessly this way and that.*

I wonder if this was the room where my mom slept, I am thinking, my chest tightening—a deep sense of being torn from something, ripped and pushed. The thought doesn't help me. I try to calm myself by unpacking my pajamas, my toiletries. My hands are shaking. I wonder if I am going to throw up.

There is a small mirror above the dresser. I peer into it. That is my face: I am still here, although I look very old. I look at my phone. I have no service, but I can feel that John and the kids are out there—their world spinning along. And I am here—separate, cut off, alone. I say aloud, "You can go home. You don't have to stay here." And I say: "That sun better not try setting or I am going to be in trouble."

I try Relaxation Jon breathing. I try counting. I stand at the window, my pulse racing, my body aching, until the sobs come and throw me onto the bed.

"I am not ready for this," I yell against the silence into my pillow. I am not ready to be *away.* I will kill myself if I have to be away like this already. I will close my eyes and hold my breath until my heart explodes. Or scream. Maybe I will scream.

I wake up hours later, and there are a few minutes of light left in the sky. I do not feel better, but I force myself to stand up, and pull on my boots. I rustle through my pill bag until I find some Xanax and I walk out the back door toward the trailhead and into the woods.

I don't walk very far. I can't. Just enough to hear my feet against the earth, the leaves crunching along the trail that traces beside a shallow creek, which is not frozen—but is very, very cold. Soon, one of the nuns rings the dinner gong, and I am able to take my weak smile and flushed cheeks and carry myself to dinner.

Later that evening I climb up to the top of the gravel road to get cell service and call John. The warm lights of the convent fill the hollow below me.

"This doesn't bode well. Even when you're not here, the kids still prefer to talk to you," says John. "Freddy keeps popping up in the doorway and then saying "oh" and going back to his room. Benny keeps hollering out your name from his bed to tell you things. Just now he yelled, 'Hey, Mom, wanna hear my top three favorite ungulates?' What am I even supposed to say to that?"

"Just say 'Absolutely,'" I say. "He doesn't care. He mainly likes to hear himself talk."

I tell him about the panic attack.

"Whoa," John says. "What are you thinking brought it on?"

It is full-on dark all around me now. I can see the nuns moving around down inside the lodge about fifty yards away.

"Being away from you guys, I guess," I say. "A sense of how much smaller my world is lately. It's intense here. Despite the cheery teal carpet, I feel like all of the world's weightiest questions have passed through these guest rooms."

I'm picturing my mom: her little black suitcase, her yoga mat, her delicate body curled in the twin bed, imagining what she still had to face.

"I'm sure they have," says John.

"I took a little walk," I tell him. "I know that's what Emerson would recommend."

The grounds here remind me a bit of Concord—farmland and woods, a forest of old hardwoods, birches and boulders, a ridge of bare branches like a wispy limbo between the earth and the sky. I could be on the paths of Walden or Estabrook if I didn't know better.

Emerson developed the pneumonia that took his life after walking too long in those woods. He was nearing eighty. "April 1882, a raw and backward spring," wrote his son Edward, the doctor—my great-great grandfather. "He caught cold and increased it by walking out in the rain and, through forgetfulness, omitting to put on his overcoat."

I picture each of these moments like cells—growing, dividing, multiplying. Emerson in the front hall; Emerson in the rain of the garden; stumbling in the woods; wet feet, forehead burning with fever by the fire, drifting in and out of sleep, pushing the embers in the grate—unsteady, a few sparks crackling and jumping forth to maybe join the greater fire—the one reaching from earth to heaven; Emerson in his bed upstairs, his body growing cold, waiting, knowing what he already knew nearly fifty years ago, and then his bones carried out through the entry.

"So what are they?" I say to John. "The three best ungulates?"

"According to Benny they are donkeys, pigs, and Spanish ibex," says John.

My chest twists with how badly I want to see them, even though it's been less than a full day. It is clear there will not be enough days. "I can't do this," I tell John. "I'm coming home tomorrow. I'm such a wimp."

"You're not though," says John. "I get it. Maybe you needed to go there to really cry."

"Maybe," I say. "And to realize I don't ever want to be away from you again until I have absolutely no choice."

"I have no problem with that," he says.

The next morning as I race toward home in the car, I feel like a spring of relief has been unearthed—a flood, the forceful waters of a birth.

28. The Ride Home

Throughout the fall, John and I take the kids to a family support group at the cancer center. The parents all meet in one room, and the kids go off for activities in another. The parents are a mixed group: lung, brain, bone, stomach, blood, skin, breast—different stages. We go around the circle and we all basically say the same thing in different ways: We are terrified. We are double terrified by how we are supposed to deal with this with our kids.

One woman, whose husband was given a few months to live but is doing well at the moment, says, "People don't get it. They think our nightmare is over because he is feeling better. But we know better. We know we are just riding the crest of the roller coaster right now."

When we meet up with the kids at the end of the night, they are hyped on new friendships and new information.

"That was awesome!" they both say, bouncing off the chairs in the lounge. "We got to learn how cancer cells grow by blowing bubbles! And we got to see real cancer on a real X-ray!"

"Did you talk at all about your experience with *my* cancer?" I ask as we walk to the parking garage.

"Sure," says Benny. "I told them it was really bad at first when you were sick all the time, but now you are much better."

Freddy stops walking and looks straight at me. "Is that right, Mom? Are you much better?"

My head is full of thick curls and I no longer am constantly going to and coming from treatment, since the trial I am on uses pills instead of infusions. I don't look like an obviously dying person—other than the cane. I've been wondering about the effect this might be having.

"I'm okay right now," I say. "But you know my cancer won't ever really get better."

They have forgotten that part. As we get in the car, I can see they are both trying not to cry.

So I climb in the back seat between them and pull each of them close to me. I haven't sat like this—John driving, me in the back beside them—since they each came home from the hospital as infants.

It's late in the evening, and we have an hour drive back to our house from the cancer center. John reaches back and squeezes my knee and then turns the music up. The boys each lean their heads on me, and we hurtle together down the dark interstate toward home.

29. Memento mori

Remember, you must die: that's the phrase that rises with me from the depths of sleep as John jumps from the hotel bed to shut off his iPhone alarm and I lie staring into the darkness while he showers. We are in Orlando, awake a half hour before sunrise. Remember you must die. From the Latin: *memento mori*.

John stumbles around filling water bottles and fumbling with the zippers on the backpacks. He brings me thin coffee in bed from a Styrofoam cup. I take a handful of ibuprofen and oxycodone. We decide it's time to wake the kids, still dead to the world in the queen bed beside ours.

Outside, the sun begins to push up over the harbor: Portofino Bay. Shapes of quiet skiffs form in the water where they have been moored for the night. A heron swoops silently over the bow of one, and then moves on.

Nuclear troupes much like ours emerge from the shadows along the empty waterfront: a mom and a dad, a couple of kids. We are quiet, mostly, shuffling toward the launch at the docks— although some, particularly the kids, are starting to pick up speed now.

We pass through security, and as we wait on the teak bench— wet and glossy with morning dew—my fingers grope through my bag and find my wallet. Inside the clasp: a stack of small cards that my fingers sort—then re-sort—by feel: park passes, early entrance passes, Express Passes, resort keys.

We are headed—like all of those around us—into the park at Universal Studios. It is the day after Christmas. It is just over a year since I was given the terminal diagnosis: a new way to mark time. *Memento mori*, I'm still saying to myself.

We have been told it is essential to be among the first to the park in order not to be stampeded by the hordes of visitors to Harry Potter's world in Diagon Alley and Hogsmeade. Freddy's plan is to purchase a wand from Ollivanders. Benny wants to track down a purple pygmy puff to go with the pink pygmy puff he has at home. They both have been told by friends that they *have to* try the Butterbeer from the red carts parked along the main drag leading up toward Hogwarts. We must hurry.

Memento mori is a term I probably first learned in one of my art history classes in Florence: the subtle skull lurking in the corner of a drawing of fruit, reminding us of our frailty and inevitable death. Both the memento mori and the vanitas—a similar concept that juxtaposed worldly things (books, wine, musical instruments) with an image of death—became hugely popular in seventeenth-century art, during a time when everyone was pretty certain that the whole point of living at all was to get to the afterlife.

The American Puritans loved the memento mori, too: my crossed-armed ancestors, who otherwise rejected art because it was considered a temptation away from God, appreciated the depic-

tions of skulls and other deathly representations as a way of embrac-
ing the notion that even in life, death is near and getting closer.

Before it was used in art, memento mori was a phrase that origi-
nated with the ancient Roman practice of a successful general returning from battle being assigned a slave to follow him around,
whispering in his ear: "*Respice post te. Hominem te memento.*"

"Look to the afterlife," the slave was instructed to say in an effort to help the general avoid haughtiness from all the praise he
received in the wake of his victory, "and remember you're only a
man." Remember, says the world—you must die.

"Keep moving," I'm saying to the kids as we step off the Hogwart's
Express and wind our way through the stanchions that will contain
the crowds who show up when they open the gates to all who do
not have special early entrance passes. "If you move quickly we
can beat the masses."

I have always been terrible at waiting in line—a trait I certainly
inherited from my mother. Even if the Express Pass and early entrance pass hadn't come included in our resort package, I would
have probably sprung for it. Or obtained the necessary paperwork
from my doctors to get one for free.

"I'll sign whatever you need," Dr. Cavanaugh said when we
told her we were surprising the boys with a trip to Universal Studios. "It's worth it—and you deserve it."

She took her kids recently. "It's such a brief window—when

they're old enough to enjoy it all and young enough to enjoy it all, too," said the busy, world-renown oncologist. "You'll have fun. You'll have a complete blast."

I've been to the real Portofino—once, on that tumultuous mother/daughter trip at age nineteen when I was learning all about memento mori. I remember the brightly painted buildings, the blue-green of the Riviera. I remember the fishing boats and the smell of coffee brewing.

I remember writing everything back to myself as we waited on the train platform—in a notebook where I had arrogantly etched *ars longa, vita brevis*: art is long, life is short. Something I had no doubt learned in a creative writing class. No wonder I had annoyed my mother so much. I remember her sitting beside me with her black backpack in her lap, working and reworking stacks of paper with her fingers: our Eurail passes, our *lire*, our map, our reserved-seat tickets. I remember the cloud of stress embanked around her:

"Don't talk to me—I'm counting! If you want to ever make it to Venice just leave me alone right now!"

Universal's Portofino Bay Hotel: a re-creation of a real Italian resort town. It's hard to keep track of the different levels of artifice here, and in some ways it reminds me of my own body. It looks intact—lovely, even, on the outside—but you can sense that on the inside something is not right.

The man-made river on which our water taxi transports us to

the main entrance of the amusement park is a little greener than blue, with just the slightest tinge of too much chemical. I try to peer into the water for fish or turtles or gators as our gleaming wood hull pushes along the canal, but I cannot see a thing.

As we glide toward the park gates, I am wondering: Does a boat captain for a real boat on a fake canal driving real people to a fake world require a real pilot's license?

King's Cross Station—where we catch the Hogwart's Express on Platform 9 3/4—is another a re-creation of a real place, with impatient crowds and a British ticket-taker and overflowing garbage cans making it entirely believable. A squirrel runs through the stiles.

"Was that a rat?" says Benny, jumping. "Do you think it's rabid?"

"What?" John exclaims. "That was a squirrel! And no, I don't think you need to worry about it being rabid."

John is on edge, and has been consumed all morning with the decision of whether or not to take a Xanax. Given my intake of pain pills, he should probably be at the top of his parenting game. But: Antianxiety meds might just be what gets him there. A bottle of them—and just about every other pill in the world—rattle around in my bag next to our stack of passes.

Hogsmeade, on the other hand, is a very realistic re-creation of a place that does not exist—except vividly in the minds of many visitors. Teenage boys stream past us in black gowns. Four-year-olds and middle-aged women stand together in front of storefronts, working out spells with wands. Freddy has emphatic opinions about restaurants: "I think we should eat at the Three Broomsticks. In the books, it's *excellent*."

The line is very long though, so instead we grab foot-long hot-dogs at a stand outside the entrance to Diagon Alley and find a place to rest our feet on some empty steps—only to be asked almost immediately if we would move for a moment by several visitors, so that they could take a picture they have traveled hundreds of miles to snap. It appears we have mistakenly stopped for lunch on the steps of the façade of the London townhome of famed Harry Potter wizard Sirius Black at 12 Grimmauld Place.

"Excuse me," says a tween in braces as she edges up next to me on the stoop. "I'm so sorry. I just really need to see if there is any chance that this door opens to somewhere."

How can you deny someone led by this instinct? I know it doesn't open, but I move my bag of potato chips out of the way. She knocks and pulls hard on the latch. After two tries, when nothing gives, she shrugs and smiles—rejoining her family and moving back into the throngs.

In the same way my fingers keep sifting through our various passes and tickets, my brain keeps trying to sort the levels of surrealness. Everywhere, quartets just like ours—and my family growing up—make their way. And in many of these little units, one member looks possibly unwell: functioning, but with something in their eyes that suggests the glimmer of the underneath.

As we thread toward the park exit that afternoon, the Minions ride has a one-hundred-and ten-minute wait—for those without an Express Pass.

"A hundred and ten minutes," says John. "That's just incredible."

He's opted against the Xanax after all, but he's feeling the high of hopping on the water taxi and heading back to Portofino Bay—the unmitigated thrill of a crowd-free afternoon.

I was here once before, when I was a year older than Freddy. Well, not here exactly—but at that esteemed amusement park down the road. Charlie was still in a stroller. I can't stop thinking about my parents. On that trip, they were a couple years older than John and I are now—yet they seemed so much more grown up: my mom stewing in stress, at every moment on the verge of yelling about the location of the traveler's checks and the free meal coupons for the Contemporary Resort. Everything a fine hair from catastrophe, checking the strapped-on wallet under her pants line with the ritual of an OCD pattern. It was not unlike our trip to Portofino.

At some level, I think travel has overall become less stressful since I was a kid—with the advent of bank cards, the euro, electronic ticketing, the iPhone. Fewer moments of stark panic on the way to the airport, at least. But maybe I am also generally less uptight of a traveler than my mom.

I am trying to know myself. I want a better sense of what kind of mother the kids will remember me to be. It's hard: I am not done becoming me. I am still in the works. I still aim to be softer in some

297

places, firmer in others. Someday—impossibly not that far from now, the boys will come to Orlando with their own families—memories etched in each of their brains of this visit here—and they will learn something of themselves, too. The shape of themselves: their arms around their kids on the teak bench, that hospital bed on the children's ward, my dad's old Datsun on the side of the highway.

As we walk together now across the Portofino piazza in the late afternoon sunset of winter, I feel us—me, John, the boys, my mom somehow—all of us hurtling separately—yet so very close to one another—toward the future.

Back at the resort pool, John and I sip real alcoholic beverages while the boys run around on a fake sand beach. We clink champagne glasses that have been specially designed not to break on the ground cover surrounding the pool, as the bartender explains to me when Freddy later knocks mine off the table with his towel.

"At least I'm here with you," I say to John—an inside joke of our relationship. *At least I'm here with you* is a line from one of the Llama Llama books that we have read to the kids before millions of bedtimes: "I think shopping's boring, too," said Little Llama's mama when the baby llama was having a meltdown in the llama version of Costco. "But at least I'm here with you." We've said it to each other a hundred times over the years—words of solidarity and disarmament on the battlefields of parenting.

What happens to little scraps like this, when there is only one person left to get the allusion? I picture a piece of paper—soggy and unreadable   that I saw a groundskeeper fish out of the canal with a net earlier in the day when we were waiting for the water taxi. What is the use of an inside joke with the dead?

"I sure wouldn't ever want to do it with anyone else," John says, putting his arm over my shoulders.

The sun on our backs is real. And Benny's laughter on his way down the pool's impressive waterslide—made to look like the ruins of an ancient temple—is real. And the boys' still-little bodies, wrapped in towels, blue-lipped and shivering in our laps after they decide the day is done: They are real.

I will never travel with my nearly grown sons through Italy. Let's just say that. Just as they will—probably—never buy an espresso with *lire* or navigate the world without a handheld map that knows their exact location and the likelihood of a coming squall to hamper their hike along the cliff side from the villages of Corniglia to Manarola. That world is gone.

Instead, we follow our children down manicured paths through an overdeveloped inland swamp, whispering *remember you must— we all must—die* in their ears as they find their way through worlds rebuilt and worlds that never were.

30. Tumor Burden

Another hospital stay—this time, my lungs. I'm not breathing well. Tests, scans, waiting. The doctors suggest a cause they are investigating: the microscopic invasion of the lymphatic ducts in the lungs of millions of unimageable cancer cells. Lymphangitic carcinomatosis. It is not a good development.

"The tumor burden could be quite high," the pulmonologist says, "making it hard to get the oxygen you need."

Tumor burden: like a backpack you might put down, like a worry you might unload, a crime you might confess. I've been here five days: the river of nurses and techs and transporters; merry-go-rounds of doctors; vitals and alarms. Someone urgently needs to weigh me at 3 a.m. Something is beeping.

Sometimes it feels like the whole world is beeping.

Outside, a dreary January morning: low clouds draped on the helicopter; uncharacteristically warm and muggy. Around noon, a hospital transporter comes for me and wheels my bed down a long corridor and into the abyss of the hospital for another breathing test, and all during our passage I can see, inside the cell-like rooms we pass, the face of the new president on dozens of TV screens. The world is anxious: The cloud cover has shifted under the tightrope. Everywhere, the tumor burden is high.

"How are you holding up today," says the breathing tech in the windowless room. "All things considered?"

I'm not sure to which things he is referring exactly. I don't know if he is sure either.

"I'm okay," I say. "Considering. How are you?"

He says he is fair to middling.

"Of course, that's what I always say," he says. "Because it about always fits."

When the scan is done, he says, "Bon voyage, madame," holding open the door as the tech wheels me back into the hallway. "*Hasta la vista.* Ta-ta for now. Have a blessed day."

When I am back in my room there is a covered tray by the bed I forgot I had ordered. There, in the chocolate pudding, I discover a continent of whipped cream that I plan to explore. And also a dish of peaches, which somehow—even in their thick syrup—are plump and firm: a suggestion of rebellion in their freshness— sweet and lovely on the tongue.

John has just returned as well—after spending a few hours at work and at home with the kids—and is now hunched in his impossible recliner by the window where he's been spending his nights, catching up on email on his laptop.

"Well, that's a mess," he is saying, sipping coffee from his thermos.

Behind John, I can see billows of steam rising off the top

of the hospital buildings, and the midday light—what there is of it—that filters through the ninth-floor window is silvery and thin.

Everything is strange—so unlike anything we have done before—and everything, too, is exactly as we imagined.

31. Scrummle

"So, do you know what 'scrummling' is?" asks Benny as we cuddle in bed on the night before I start a new chemo regimen. Downstairs: the sound of our new at-home oxygen compressor—kicking on, kicking off. I don't yet need the extra air in bed.

I'm on the laptop, searching unsuccessfully on the regular Internet forums for people's experiences with the cocktail. Then it occurs to me that I'm not finding much because generally these people are pretty dead. It's not like with the earlier drugs where everyone's buzzing about hair loss and metallic tongue.

"I do not," I say. "Do you?"

"Sure. It's a secret sound," he says. "A puppy sound. Only puppies can hear it. And you and I are brand-new puppies who haven't opened our eyes and only know how to scrummle."

"Does MacDuff know about scrummling?" I ask MacDuff on the floor.

"He used to," Benny tells me. "But he might have forgotten now."

"Now that you mention it," I say to him, closing my laptop and snuggling us both down deep under the covers, "I think I *do* remember scrummling. From when you were a baby."

"That would make sense," says Benny. "It's a being-born sound."

No sound that feels farther away to me these days than a being-born sound. Here in our waning thirties, some of my closest contemporaries are having babies. My best friend from high school is about to give birth to her fourth. Bonnie and her girlfriend have hatched a plan to conceive. My mom was pregnant with Charlie when she was exactly as old as I am now. It feels impossible, as my days are filled with imagining how to wind things down, that someone my age is winding things up, preparing new life, getting ready to scrummle.

"It's kind of a digging sound," Benny tells me. "Like *scrumma scrumma scrumma, scrumma scrumma scrumma.* Like you're moving toward something, even though you're already happy where you are."

"Oh yes, I definitely know that sound," I say. "Can you do it even when you're not really a newborn puppy?"

"Only if you know the secret," he whispers. "That you're not really moving anywhere. You just make it look like you are to someone who isn't paying close attention."

32. The Bright Hour

According to Freddy, the apocalypse has come. Today is his birthday—ten—and despite my passionate resistance over the last decade to gun play, we have given him the granddaddy of weapons: the Nerf N-Strike Elite Demolisher 2-in-1 Blaster, a semiautomatic, batteries-required, 2-in-1 missile-launching, cartridge-loading blaster that is so heavy it needs a strap.

"Seriously, Mom—this is basically world ending. Who even are you anymore?" Freddy says when he rips off the wrapping paper at the breakfast table.

For the first time since I have been home from the hospital, the sun is out: a warm, health-filled, spring-will-come, balm of a sun. After school, I denounce homework (birthday, sun) and the boys holler and mud-kick out into the wide yard with the Great Demolisher and some lesser demolishers. I am still short of breath and weak, but I come sit on the steps of the back deck in a T-shirt and sweat pants and feel the light on my skin: There is life—this bright hour. *Let us make good use of time,* whispers Montaigne.

"What are you guys pretending?" I ask when the boys come panting to a stop for a moment by my side.

"Well, I am the leader of a rogue posse of survivors after a devastating nuclear tsunami has wiped out most of the world," Freddy says. He is dressed up in his Slash leather jacket from Halloween, aviator sunglasses, a self-styled balaclava, snow boots—and of course the Demolisher. "Benny is my executive assistant revolutionary and we are trying to get to a safe haven in the tree house where our comrades have sent signals that there is a food supply."

"Yikes," I say. "Sounds intense."

Benny yells "*Nuclear tsunami!*" and leaps off the steps next to me, thrusting a sword into the air. In his other hand he is somehow carrying a notebook, an extra Nerf gun, and a stuffed turkey vulture.

I can hear through the open window that John has come home from work—rustling in the kitchen, maybe with the birthday cake.

"I'm on the deck," I call out.

"Okay," he calls back. "I'll be out there in just a sec."

Something in his voice—*just a sec*—a sliver of impatience, an edge—makes me flash to our voices that taut night in the bedroom not long after I was diagnosed. My voice: I have to love these days the same as any other. His voice: I'm so afraid I can't breathe.

We're making our way like this, though: We are breathless, but we love the days. They are promises. They are the only way to walk from one night to the other.

Already, the boys are off to the wilds again—whooping and surviving. It will be getting dark soon—the sky has started with that eerie postapocalyptic light of a warm evening in winter—but I am not ready to call them back in. There is nothing in this whole world that could make me call them back in.

Afterword

Nina completed the manuscript for *The Bright Hour* in late January 2017. By then, we knew the cancer had spread significantly in her lungs. Her prognosis was grim. While working on the final edits of the book, she became weaker, her breathing difficult and labored, even at rest. She was admitted to Duke University Hospital on February 16. Later that week, after discussing the remaining treatment options with her oncologist, Nina decided to enter a hospice facility in Greensboro, five minutes from our home, rather than pursue an aggressive course of chemotherapy that seemed more likely to shorten her life than marginally prolong it.

As the sun set on Saturday, February 25, Jennie and Bonnie took the boys home for dinner. They said good night to Nina, not goodbye. After midnight Nina's breathing changed. I called her father and brother, who came out to sit vigil with me through the night. In my delirium and grief, I had flashes of Nina when she was in labor with Freddy ten years before.

Morning was always Nina's favorite time of day. Before she got sick, she used to bounce out of bed at first light, and she insisted on open blinds when we went to bed, even if we were in a hotel with an eastern exposure in the desert. So it seemed fitting that she died at 6 a.m. on February 26, just before the sun came up.

—JOHN DUBERSTEIN, MARCH 2017

Acknowledgments

Nina really wanted to be around to see *The Bright Hour* go to press. But, while she did not live to see the book materialize fully, she died knowing it was in production and was keenly grateful to a great number of folks who made that possible.

Nina's agent at The Book Group, Brettne Bloom, is an astonishingly kind, talented, warm, and powerful human being. Having Brettne as an agent was like finding a sister Nina never knew she had. Lasting friendships sometimes do not get to last, sadly, but there's no doubt that Nina and Brettne had already established the foundations of one.

Nina also wanted to thank her editor at Simon & Schuster, Marysue Rucci. When we met with Brettne and Marysue in Greensboro, I could not believe that Nina had the good fortune to be involved professionally with *both* these women. I suppose it makes sense that Nina's dream agent would obtain for her the perfect editor. Marysue not only took on the project of a dying woman, with all its inherent risks (noncompletion, for one), but made Nina feel as vital as any author— sick or well—could in the writing of a manuscript. She too forged a relationship with Nina that transcended their professional roles.

During what would prove Nina's only visit to New York and the Simon & Schuster offices, she was celebrated by her team at S&S before she'd even completed the work. Marysue had laid the groundwork, but a whole mess of Simon & Schuster folks followed suit, including: Carolyn Reidy, Jonathan Karp, Richard Rhorer,

Acknowledgments

Cary Goldstein, Sarah Reidy, Dana Trocker, Ebony LaDelle, Martha Schwartz, Carly Loman, Jackie Seow, Thomas Colligan, and Lisa Rivlin. Special thanks to Zack Knoll at S&S and Dana Murphy at The Book Group for their wonderful work behind the scenes.

Nina wanted to thank Samantha Hahn for the fantastic cover art, and Jenny Meyer, who handled Nina's foreign rights. She was also incredibly grateful to all her foreign publishers, especially Australian publisher Michael Heyward and his lovely colleagues at Text, whose encouragement and feedback were much appreciated during the writing process. Also Michelle Weiner at CAA.

Thanks to Dan Jones at the *New York Times'* Modern Love column for publishing her piece, "When a Couch Is More than a Couch," a dream publication for Nina and one that led directly to this book. Nina also wanted to thank Drew Perry, whose insightful edits were almost all incorporated into the book; Tita Ramirez; Melissa and Adam Tarleton; Heidi Levine; Amanda Moore, who read drafts of what would become *The Bright Hour*; and Cristina Henriquez, who advised Nina early on about how to develop a book project. Nina had the support of a very close circle throughout her life and her illness, including my sister Jennie Duberstein; Nina's cousin Bonnie Dundee; her best friend since high school Eliza Harrington Myers; her brother, Charlie Riggs, and his wife, Amelia; and her father, Peter Riggs, the kindest, most supportive, and most quietly competent parent a girl could hope for and one of the best human beings I have ever met. Nina couldn't share *The Bright Hour* with her mom, Jan Riggs, who passed away in August 2015. Nina's resolve and clarity in the face of terminal disease is an implicit tribute to her mom, who was a source of much of Nina's strength and clarity on mortality.

Nina was also enormously grateful to Dr. Cavanaugh and Dr. Rosenblum at the Duke Cancer Center. Wherever she went, it seemed, Nina was attended by badass professional women. Speaking of badass women, fathomless gratitude to Nina's friend Virginia Darden Meeks, or just Ginny. Ginny was diagnosed about the same time as Nina with the same crappy triple negative breast cancer, and died three days before, as Nina lay in hospice. When I told Nina about Ginny's death, it hit her harder than just about anything. Ginny was a fierce, hilarious, and lovely person. The kids Ginny left behind and the friendships she helped to create between our family and hers are gift enough, but knowing her also made Nina's journey through the stygian realms of metastatic breast cancer a whole lot brighter.

Lastly, although we talked about *The Bright Hour* being Nina's legacy to our kids, Freddy and Benny—and I hope it will through successive readings help them to know her and understand the love she had for them better as they get older—I'm sure Nina wanted to thank the two of them and me. We were a heck of a little unit and the work of her adult life was actually much more about sowing the seeds of future happiness for us than it was about writing. Happily, I think she managed to do both. No dedication can describe how much I love or miss her, but I am also really grateful for everything she did to prepare us for this tremendous loss and all she left behind, especially this chronicle and our two boys.

—JOHN DUBERSTEIN

About the Author

NINA RIGGS received her MFA in poetry in 2004 and published a book of poems, *Lucky, Lucky,* in 2009. She wrote about life with metastatic breast cancer on her blog, *Suspicious Country*; her recent work has appeared in the *Washington Post* and the *New York Times.* She lived with her husband and sons and dogs in Greensboro, North Carolina.